MOUNTAIN STIRRINGS

MOUNTAIN STIRRINGS

A Cookbook By The Chefs Of The Northshire

Marshall Jones Co.
Manchester Center, Vermont
Publishers Since 1902
In collaboration with...
Editorial Concepts, Inc.
Manchester Center, Vermont

Library of Congress Catalog Card Number 94-077842

I.S.B.N. 0-8338-0213-5

Printed in the United States of America

For Our Northshire Guests.

With appreciation and an invitation to return
and visit us again and again.

STIR*RING; as an adjective.
Exciting strong feelings, as of inspiration.

We've all said it dozens of times. We sip our coffee, satisfied and pleased with a truly wonderful dining experience. "You know," you say to your companion, "I wish I could prepare and serve this entire dinner — appetizer to desert — for us at home. We could even invite the Smiths."

"Right," says our companion. "And, perhaps we could paint our hills green as well."

Welcome to *MOUNTAIN STIRRINGS, A Cookbook By The Chefs Of The Northshire.* Here is a collection of some 30 *complete meals* you can indeed prepare in *your* kitchen just for you and your guests. Each menu is carefully presented by *The Chefs Of The Northshire.* Enjoy our unique cookbook. Learn the stories behind the inns, hotels and restaurants. Meet the chefs, up close and personal. And, start your personal inspirational *Mountain Stirrings.*

The northern portion of the Shire *(in this case, the Shire is Bennington County, Vermont)* is well known as *Manchester & The Mountains,* the vacation center of Southern Vermont. Ours is a beautiful region, renowned for its sense of history, its fine inns, places to dine, to ski , golf, play tennis, hike, fish, bicycle, shop and to be culturally, physically and emotionally enriched. Now, you can take a little bite of *The Northshire* home with you.

MOUNTAIN STIRRINGS is joint production of two Northshire firms, *Editorial Concepts, Inc.,* a book packaging company, Paul Wheeler, President and the *Marshall Jones Co.*, an old New England publishing enterprise, Peggi F. Simmons, Publisher and Craig A. Altschul, Editor. Cover photography by Dorset photographer Cook Neilson, with illustrations by Dorset Artist Lindy Bowden. *(Thanks, too, for produce for our cover from the Village Green Grocer and fresh bread from Al Ducci's Italian Pantry, styled for Cook's camera by Stepp Neilson.)*

We gratefully acknowledge the chefs, innkeepers, restauranteurs and hoteliers who have made this special cookbook possible. A portion of the proceeds from sales of the book will help to establish or augment cookbook sections of local school and public libraries. *Bon Appetit.*

On The Menu

2. Cool Autumn Evening

Wilburton Focaccia
Savory Portabello Tart
Boston Bibb Lettuce With Mustard Maple Dressing
Oven Roasted Duckling With Cointreau Orange Sauce, Wild Rice
Caramel Custard

Please note: All menus are for four persons unless otherwise stated in recipes.

The Barrows House

"More Like A Home Than An Inn"

The Barrows House is an historic inn of eight buildings nestled on 12 park-like acres in Dorset. It's white clapboarded buildings, old-fashioned colorful gardens, manicured lawns and stately trees all evoke a sense of history which can be traced to the founding days of the town itself in the 1700s.

The grounds actually belonged to the Dorset Church in 1784 and the first church was built near one corner of the property. The main house was built for the colorful Rev. William Jackson, the second pastor. Experience and Theresa Barrows purchased the property in 1888 and established it as an inn.

Since that time, the Barrows House has been operated by five consecutive families. Purchased by Jim and Linda McGinnis in 1993, the Barrows House continues to provide a haven of hospitality that is, in Experience Barrows words, more like a home than an inn.

The Barrows House is truly an inn for all seasons and reasons. It's unique facilities and grounds make it a special place for family gatherings, honeymoons, small business meetings or spur-of-the-moment vacations. There is a feeling of a time gone by, yet with all comfortable, modern conveniences. Each of the rooms, cottages and sitting areas are uniquely furnished with antiques, old family pieces and modern bedding. For several Sunday afternoons in early summer the Barrows House presents *The Littlest Music Festival,* a series of benefit concerts for the Manchester Food Cupboard, on the gazebo lawn.

Among the many Barrows House pleasures is the excellent gourmet kitchen. Using the freshest ingredients available during all seasons, Chef Gary Walker and his staff create memorable meals that bring guests back for many visits. Breakfast and dinner is served every day, with snacks and light lunches available poolside in season.

The Barrows House, Route 30, Dorset, Vermont 05251
(802) 867-4455, (800) 639-1620 (out-of-state)

1. Swordfish At The Barrows

On The Menu

Phyllo Wrapped Brie, Apples and Scallions on Raspberry Coulis
Smoked Tomato Vinaigrette
Grilled Swordfish with Roasted Corn and Tomato Relish
Walnut Lace Cookie Cups with Lemon Curd and Fresh Berries

Phyllo Wrapped Brie, Apples and Scallions on Raspberry Coulis

Phyllo:
6 oz Brie *(cut into 4 pieces)*
1 large Granny Smith apple *(diced)*
1/8 cup scallions *(sliced)*
1 tbls raspberry vinegar
6 phyllo dough sheets
½ cup melted butter
Raspberry Coulis:
1 pint raspberries
1 tbls raspberry vinegar
1 tbls sugar
1 tsp orange rind

Sauté apples and scallions with the raspberry vinegar for 5 minutes. Remove from heat. Don't overcook the apples and make sure they are firm, not crisp. Set aside.

Lay one phyllo sheet out on a work table. *(It dries out quickly.)* With a pastry brush, spread the butter over the dough generously. Then top with another sheet of dough and paint again with butter. Repeat until you have 3 sheets. Cut the 3 sheets in half and then fold the sheets in half. Place Brie, apples and scallions in the phyllo fold and wrap the Brie, applying more butter if needed. Repeat process. May be made ahead.

Cook all ingredients for *coulis* over low heat until thoroughly cooked. Put in blender or food processor and strain. Leave at room temperature.

Bake Brie packets in a 350 degree pre-heated oven for 10-15 minutes until phyllo is golden brown. Turn once or twice so they do not burn on bottom. Place raspberry coulis on plate with baked Brie on top and garnish with fresh vegetables for four servings.

Smoked Tomato Viniagrette Dressing

2 large smoked tomatoes
¾ cup champagne vinegar
1 diced shallot
3 cups olive oil
salt and pepper

Purée tomatoes in blender and strain. Put in stainless steel bowl. Add shallots and vinegar. Whisk in oil slowly. Add salt and pepper as desired. Use with various combination salads of fresh greens and raw vegetables.

Grilled Swordfish With Roasted Corn And Tomato Relish

4, 6 oz swordfish steaks
2 ears corn *(roasted with husk on and removed from cob)*
2 tomatoes *(peeled, skinned and diced)*
1 clove garlic *(diced)*
1 small jalapeno pepper *(diced)*
½ small red onion *(diced)*
½ small red bell pepper *(diced)*
1 tsp cumin
1 tsp chili powder
1 tsp red pepper *(ground)*
1 tsp fresh cilantro
1 tbls lime juice
1 tbls champagne vinegar

Mix all relish ingredients together. Season with salt and pepper to taste. Grill swordfish to desired doneness. Top with relish and serve. This recipe is heart-healthy and delicious.

Walnut Lace Cookies With Lemon Curd And Fresh Berries

¼ cup light brown sugar
2 tbls light corn syrup
3 tbls unsalted butter
¼ tsp salt
¼ cup all purpose flour
¼ cup chopped walnuts

In heavy saucepan, combine brown sugar, corn syrup, butter and salt and bring to a boil, whisking. When butter is melted, remove from heat, add flour and walnuts and mix well. Place four, one-tbls portions of cookie dough about 6 inches apart on greased cookie sheet. Bake at 350 degrees for 5-8 minutes, or until golden. Remove from oven, let cool for 3 minutes, until set, but flexible. Remove with thin spatula, drape over inverted custard cups. Let set, then gently remove.

Lemon curd:
5 egg yolks
½ cup sugar
6 tbls butter
¼ cup fresh lemon sauce
1 tbls lemon zest

Combine all ingredients in heavy saucepan. Bring to slow boil, whisking continuously to prevent scorching. Cook about 20 minutes, until thick. Curd will continue to firm up as it cools. Garnish with fresh berries.

Wine Suggestion

Chardonnay, Edna Valley

2. Dine On Hazlenut Salmon

On The Menu

Maine Crab Cakes Chesapeake Style
Salad With Maple Mustard Dressing
Hazlenut Mustard Encrusted Salmon With Sundried Tomatoes And Dill
Chocolate Amaretto Mousse Meringue Nests

Maine Crab Cakes Chesapeake Style

(Yield: 6-8, 2 inch crabcakes)

¾ cup mayonnaise
3 eggs
4 slices fresh white bread *(processed to medium fine crumbs)*
2 tbls Old Bay Seasoning
1 tbls dry mustard
1 tbls fresh chives *(chopped)*
1 tsp dry oregano *(or 1 tbls fresh, chopped oregano)*
1 tsp dry basil *(or 1 tbls fresh, chopped basil)*
½ medium red pepper
½ medium spanish onion *(diced small)*
1 lb crabmeat

Mix first 8 ingredients together until well blended. Sauté pepper and onion in a little butter until soft. Add to mayonnaise mixture. Gently fold in crabmeat. Shape into 2 inch patties. Sauté in butter at medium high heat to brown both sides.

Sauce for crabcakes:
1 tbls flour
1 tbls butter
1 cup heavy cream
1 tbls Old Bay Seasoning
2 dashes tabasco

Melt butter in medium saucepan. Add flour and stir. Add rest of ingredients. Cook over medium heat, stirring, until mixture thickens.

Maple Mustard Dressing for Salad

½ cup maple syrup
½ cup Dijon mustard *(grainy, country style)*
¼ cup champagne vinegar
1½ cup salad oil
salt and pepper

Mix first three ingredients and then add salad oil in a slow, steady stream, whisking constantly. Add salt and pepper to taste.

Hazlenut Mustard Encrusted Salmon With Sun Dried Tomatoes And Dill

Whip together:
1 egg
½ cup mustard
Mix together:
1 cup bread crumbs
1 cup hazlenuts *(finely ground)*

Dredge 4 portions of salmon in 1½ cups flour, then egg mixture and then crumb and nut mixture. Sauté in butter until brown. Turn and brown other side. Place in 350 degree oven for 7-10 minutes.

Meanwhile, make sauce:
3 tbls vermouth
1 tbls sun-dried tomatoes *(finely chopped)*
2 tbls heavy cream
3 tbls butter *(cubed)*
½ tsp fresh dill *(chopped)*

Reduce vermouth and tomatoes until nearly dry. Add cream. Bring to boil. Whisk in butter. Add dill. Adjust salt and pepper. Pour over salmon when serving.

Chocolate Amaretto Mousse Meringue Nests

Chocolate Mousse Filling:
3 cups heavy cream
½ cup Amaretto
1½ lb semi-sweet chocolate
1½ cups egg yolks
½ lb sugar

Whip heavy cream until almost stiff. Add Amaretto. Set aside. Melt chocolate in double boiler. Set aside. Whip egg yolks and sugar until fluffy. Slowly add melted chocolate until well mixed. Fold whipped cream into chocolate mixture. Chill until set.

Meringue Nests:
4 egg whites
1 cup sugar
¼ tsp salt
¼ tsp cream of tartar
4 tsp cornstarch
1 tsp vanilla
1 tsp champagne vinegar

Whip egg whites until frothy. Add salt and cream of tartar. Continue whipping until almost stiff and slowly add sugar. Continue whipping and add cornstarch, then vinegar and vanilla. Spoon into pastry bag fitted with star tip. Pipe nests onto a parchment or waxed paper covered cookie sheet. Place in a very low heated oven

(100 degrees) and let dry. Check occasionally to be sure they are not browning. If they are, turn off heat completely and let set overnight.

Wine Suggestion

Graves, Chateau de Chantegrive

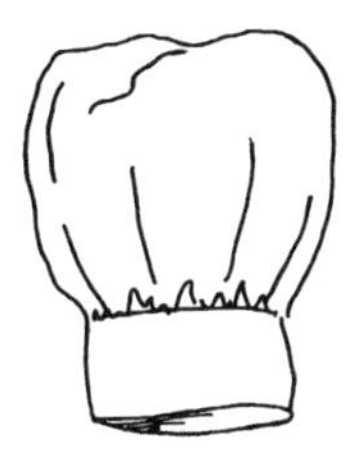

Meet The Barrows House Chef Gary Walker

Gary Walker is head chef at The Barrows House and has been literally in the restaurant business since age 16. His mother, a waitress, introduced him to the restaurant world, and he began by washing dishes and busing tables, soon working his way up to line and assistant chef.

After earning an associate degree in hotel management at Brandywine Jr. College, he worked at the Ramada Inn in Wilmington, Delaware. There, he worked under Les Pack, who taught him the secrets of soups and stocks. Gary's impressive repertoire of soups got their start at the Ramada and continue to grow.

He went on to spend six years at the Hercules Country Club as sous chef, working on a variety of member functions, banquets and a la carte dining. Next came a family enterprise, the Victorian Rose restaurant, also in Wilmington. Then, on to the Northeast River Yacht Club as sous chef.

Moving to Vermont in 1988, Gary became the chef at the Inn at Willow Pond and came to the Barrows House six years ago as sous chef working with Chefs Tim Blackwell and Ken Paquin.

He describes the Barrows House cuisine as Regional American and he uses the finest available ingredients. For example, his famed Maine Crabcakes Chesapeake Style are offered as both appetizers and as main menu entreés because of guests requests. *(That recipe is included).* It all proves you can take the man out of Delaware, but you can't take those wonderful ways of Delaware cooking out of the man.

Not resting on his accomplishments, Gary is studying for his bachelors degree at Castleton State College in business and computer science.

Gary and his wife, Claudia, are Dorset residents. Their sons Gregory and Geoffrey, Dorset Elementary School students, are regular visitors to the Barrows House kitchen and have become expert food critics. Gary says the specialize in desserts.

Bistro Henry

A Restaurant For Today

Bistro Henry is a restaurant for today. Owned & operated by acclaimed chefs Henry and Dina Bronson, Bistro Henry serves breakfast, Sunday brunch and dinner,with menus that have something for everyone!

Easily accessible on Route 11/30, the Bromley Mountain Road *(at the Chalet Motel)*, Bistro Henry is reasonably priced, with today's value conscious diner in mind. A meal at Bistro Henry will be a highlight of your visit to the Northshire.

Henry and Dina take great pride in using fresh and fine ingredients and serving them in a friendly, casual dining room where guests will be comfortable in anything from jeans to evening wear.

Because a guest's comfort and pleasure are the Bistro Henry priorities, special needs and diets are accommodated whenever possible.

For the younger set (under 12), there is a delightful Children's Menu featuring favorites like grilled cheese, hamburgers, hot dogs, pasta with tomato sauce (or just butter) including a salad, beverage, french fries (where appropriate), and ice cream.

Look for daily specials, Dina's exquisite desserts, a full bar and extensive Wine List (with emphasis on high quality/reasonable prices) to complete the offerings.

So...come visit Bistro Henry for some of the finest food and service in Southern Vermont.

Bistro Henry, Routes 11/30 At The Chalet Motel,
Manchester Center, Vermont 05255 (802) 362-4982

1. Mediterranean Vegetarian Feast

On The Menu

Tian of Mushroom & Potatoes with Goat Cheese
Mixed Greens with Balsamic Vinaigrette
Eggplant Terrine, Sauce Provençale & Pasta
Lemon Sorbet

Tian of Mushroom & Potatoes with Goat Cheese

1/2 lb mushrooms *(sliced & sautéed in a little olive oil)*
1 lb new potatoes
1 tbls Dijon mustard
2 shallots *(chopped)*
2 oz sherry vinegar
½ cup extra virgin olive oil
1 tsp each chopped fresh parsley, chervil & chives
salt & pepper
8 oz goat cheese *(sliced...Vermont Chèvre is perfect)*
3 oz heavy cream *(reduced until thickened)*
Chervil sprigs, diced tomato, Niçoise olives for garnish

Cook potatoes in their skins, in salted water until tender. Meanwhile, combine mustard, shallots, vinegar in a non-reactive bowl. Whisk in oil. Stir in herbs. Adjust salt & pepper.

Peel potatoes while hot *(hold them with a cloth or dip your hand in ice water often).* Cut them in ½ inch cubes. Toss with the dressing to start. Use more if potatoes really soak it up. Save a little for the finished dish.

Preheat oven to 400 degrees. Set up a baking sheet with 4 ring molds that have been well oiled. Put a layer of potatoes in the bottom of the mold, then a layer of mushrooms, then potatoes, then mushrooms. Finish with the cheese. Brush cheese with reduced cream. Bake tians for 10 minutes, just to warm. Finish under broiler to brown the cheese. With a spatula, transfer the rings to plates. Garnish with chervil, tomato & olives. Drizzle a little remaining vinaigrette around tian.

Mixed Greens with Balsamic Vinaigrette

1 small head Boston lettuce
1 bunch watercress
½ head leaf lettuce
¼ cup best aged Balsamic vinegar
1 cup Extra Virgin olive oil
salt and freshly ground black pepper

Tear, wash and dry greens in the usual manner. Combine oil and vinegar. Adjust seasoning. Toss greens with enough dressing to lightly coat. Reserve excess. Divide among four plates.

Eggplant Mushroom Terrine

5 lb eggplant *(peeled, sliced length-wise in ¼ inch thick slices)*
1.5 lb mushrooms *(sliced ¼ inch thick)*
½ lb Swiss cheese *(grated)*
1.5 cups half & half
3 eggs plus 1 yolk
2 tsp vegetable oil
butter for greasing pan
9x5x4 non-reactive loaf pan and parchment paper

Lay slices of eggplant on a rack. Dust liberally with Kosher salt. Let sit at least 1 hour to allow bitterness to leach out. Sauté mushrooms *(in oil)* long enough so that nearly all the moisture is gone. I prefer to preheat pan, add mushrooms, cook a few minutes, then add the oil. Season with salt & pepper. Preheat grill. Oil lightly with oil soaked cloth. Grill eggplant slices on both sides until nicely marked and just done- about 2-3 minutes per side depending on heat of fire. Allow to cool. Beat eggs & yolk. Stir in Half & Half. Season with salt & pepper.

To assemble: Brush pan with butter. Line with parchment paper so that enough is left to fold back over to cover top. Apply a layer of eggplant slices, 1 or 2 slices thick, depending on overall thickness of cooked eggplant. Add a layer of mushrooms, about ¼. Sprinkle with Swiss cheese, about ¼. Pour over approximately ¼ of egg mixture. Apply next layer of eggplant and press down. Repeat steps 3-5 until all ingredients are used. Be sure to finish with eggplant only. Cover with parchment, then aluminum foil.

Bake at 375 degrees approximately 1¾ - 2 hours or until set nicely. Allow to cool completely *(ideally refrigerated)*. Invert onto cutting board to un mold. Peel off paper and slice in 1inch thick slices. Reheat at 450 degrees for approximately 7 minutes. Serve with pasta Sauce Provençale, and green vegetable such as spinach, broccoli or zucchini.

Sauce Provençale

1, 28 oz can diced tomatoes
½ cup fresh basil *(coarsely chopped)*
¼ cup extra virgin olive oil
6 cloves garlic *(sliced thin)*
1/2 tsp. crushed red pepper
1/4 cup pitted Greek olives or Niçoise olives *(preferred)*
salt to taste

In non-reactive pot, cook tomatoes *(fast enough so that they do not stick and burn, but not so slow that they take forever)* until they are a nice and thick sauce-like consistency. 1-1½ hours. This also concentrates flavor and cooks away any excessive acidity. When tomatoes are ready, remove from fire. Sauté garlic in ½ of the oil until just barely starting to brown. Add red pepper and olives. Cook 3-4 more minutes. Add to tomatoes. Add remaining oil and basil to sauce. Allow to cool. Reheat as needed.

Lemon Sorbet

5 oz fresh lemon juice
½ cup water
1 cup sugar syrup *(combine 1½ cups sugar with 1 cup water, boil, cook 2 minutes. Let cool)*
zest of 1 lemon
berries and/or mint for garnish

In shallow pan, combine ingredients *(except for berries/garnish)*. Place in freezer. Stir every 4 hours to break up ice chunks. Freeze at least overnight. 1 hour before serving, process in food processor until smooth. Re-freeze until serving. Serve in chilled glasses, garnished with mint and berries. *Alternative:* Prepare sorbet in ice cream machine following manufacturer's instructions.

Wine Suggestions

Domaine de la Moutète, Cotes De Provence Rosé; Bourgeuil, Marcel Martin, 1990; Beaujolais Villages, Duboeuf, 1992 and Chateau Perenne, Cotes du Blaye, 1989

2. An Easy Winter Feast

On The Menu

Onion Soup Gratinée
Greens with Walnut & Roquefort
Steak au Poivre Bistro Henry
Warm Gingerbread with Apples & Caramel

Onion Soup Gratinée

1 lb white onion *(thinly sliced)*
1 cup sherry
1 cup dry white wine
2 tbls butter
1 quart beef broth *(preferably homemade)*
4-8 slices toasted French bread
2 cups Swiss or Gruyère cheese *(grated)*
2 oz of your finest port
2 eggs

In large non-reactive sauté pan, melt butter and sauté onions on medium-high fire until brown and tender, about 15 minutes. Add sherry and wine and simmer until nearly evaporated, about another 10 minutes. Meanwhile, bring the stock to a boil, then add to onions. Simmer 3 minutes. Season with salt and pepper.

Preheat Broiler. Divide soup among 4 oven proof soup crocks. Top with bread slices *(enough to cover most of the soup).* Cover bread with the cheese and broil until brown & bubbly, about 5 minutes. Meanwhile, beat eggs with the port. When the soup is ready, divide the egg-port mixture among the bowls by lifting the cheese with a fork and stirring a little into each bowl of soup.

Greens with Walnut Vinaigrette & Roquefort

3 cups, Romaine, Radicchio, and Leaf Lettuce (washed and dried)
2 tbls fresh lemon juice
1 shallot *(minced)*
¼ cup walnut or hazelnut oil
salt & freshly ground pepper
1 cup walnuts, toasted & lightly salted
4 oz. Roquefort cheese *(the genuine article is the best!)*

Combine lemon, shallot, oil in non-reactive bowl. Adjust seasoning. Toss greens with dressing. Divide among 4 salad plates. Sprinkle with walnuts and crumbled cheese.

Steak au Poivre Bistro Henry

4, 10 oz Strip, Tenderloin, Bottom Butt Sirloin Steaks
1 ½ tbls black peppercorns, crushed *(use the bottom of a skillet and roll over them or pound between several layers of wax paper)*
salt
1 tbls butter
2 shallots *(chopped)*
½ cup beef stock, preferably homemade
1 tsp cornstarch dissolved in 2 tsp water
¼ cup Cognac
¼ cup heavy cream
1 tsp Dijon mustard

Preheat a skillet large enough to hold all the steaks. Press the pepper into each steak. Salt lightly. Bring the stock to a boil and thicken lightly with cornstarch slurry. Add the butter, then the steaks. Cook for a few minutes per side for medium rare. Remove steaks and keep warm. Add shallots, cook 2 minutes. Add Cognac, cook down 1-3 minutes. Add cream and reduce by 50 percent. Add stock, then mustard. Cook until nice sauce consistency is reached. Adjust salt and pepper. Pour over steaks. Serve with French fried potatoes or a potato gratin and a vegetable such as string beans.

Gingerbread with Sautéed Apples (or Pears)

9x13 baking pan, buttered & floured
Oven, preheat to 375 degrees
6 oz butter at room temp.
6 oz brown sugar

3 eggs
6 oz molasses
12 oz warm beer *(preferably dark)*
1 oz candied ginger *(chopped finely)*
zest of 1 lemon *(grated)*

Sift together the following dry ingredients:

12 oz. flour
1 tsp baking soda
1 tsp ground cinnamon
1 tsp ground ginger
½ tsp salt
½ tsp nutmeg

Cream butter & sugar until fluffy. Add eggs 1 at a time, beating constantly. Stir in 1/3 of dry mixture. Add molasses and ½ of the beer. Mix until blended. Stir in 1/3 of dry mixture. Add remaining beer. Stir in remaining dry mixture. Fold in ginger & lemon zest. *(Mixture may look curdled! Fear not!)* Scrape into prepared pan. Bake approximately 35 minutes or until center springs back when touched lightly.

3 Granny Smith Apples or Bosc Pears *(peeled, cored & cut into large chunks)*
½ cup sugar
juice of ½ lemon
2 tblsp butter

Preheat sauté pan *(dry)* over medium heat. Add apples, butter and sauté until they begin to color. Add the sugar & lemon juice. Continue cooking until apples are caramelized. Keep warm.

Caramel Sauce:
1 cup sugar
¾ cup water
½ cup heavy cream

In small heavy bottomed saucepan, combine sugar and water. Cook over high heat, stirring until mixture comes to a boil. Continue cooking over high heat, until sugar reaches deep caramel color. Remove from fire and add cream in thin stream. *(Be careful!)* Mixture will bubble and give off live steam. When bubbles subside, stir and return to fire until homogenized. Keep warm. *To serve:* Cut gingerbread in 2" squares. Place in center of dessert plate. Dust with Confectioner's sugar. Spoon apples on one side and sauce on other. Garnish with a little whipped cream and mint leaf.

Wine Suggestions:

Karly Zinfandel, 1988, Beaulieu Cabernet Sauvignon, 1990, Chateau Romefort, Haut Médoc, 1989, Chateau Simard, St. Emilion, 1983

Meet Bistro Henry Chefs
Henry & Dina Bronson

Bistro Henry is truly the story of Henry and Dina Bronson, who have put their talents together for the second time in Manchester. They met in the kitchens of Manhattan's finest restaurants and brought their dream to Vermont in 1988, when they opened Dina's. After four successful years, their search for greener pastures and desire to spend more time with their one year old daughter, Talia, brought them to the decision to close Dina's in October 1992.

As fortune would have it, rather than reopen Dina's, they discovered the perfect spot for *Bistro Henry* - which they consider a restaurant for today.

Drawing on nearly 20 years experience (including 1½ years living and dining in France) Henry has put together an authentic French Bistro menu, elevating the classics to the more modern style of the 90's. Dina collaborates on the menu, expertly guides the service staff and creates the exquisite desserts - including the finest crème brulée anywhere.

Dina's Manhattan cooking experience includes Delectable, Safari Grill, Cafe Marimba, Brasserie Bijou, Metropolis, Soho Kitchen and Bar and Huberts. She is an Honor Graduate of the New York Cooking Center and the State University of New York, College at Oneonta where she holds a BA in Theatre and Literature in Highest Honors.

Henry's New York City and State restaurant resume includes Salvucci's and the Reservoir Inn, West Hurley; Dutchess Manor, Beacon; Pig Heaven, Safari Grill, Cafe Marimba, Mumbles, Voulez Vous in Manhattan.

Dina and Henry look forward to having you join them again and again.

The Black Swan

An Historical Farm; An Elegant Restaurant

Known to so many as the Munson Farm, the house that has become *The Black Swan* restaurant sits upon land that was originally part of a huge tract in Manchester Village, including what is now the 1811 House. The Munsons obtained this land from the Burtons, some of the original Manchester settlers and also their cousins.

Cyrus Munson and his first wife built the brick house in 1834. After she passed away in 1841, he remarried the same year and his only child, Loveland, was born in 1843. Cyrus was active in the Manchester community and was a trustee of Burr & Burton Seminary from 1829 until his death in 1857.

Loveland was a brilliant boy, but had to take over working the farm at age 14, when his father died. He finished his education, studied law, became editor of the Manchester Journal during the Civil War and later served in the Vermont Legislature. He became a Chief Justice of the Vermont Supreme Court in 1917. Loveland was an avid historian and excellent speaker.

The farm was sold to Ivan and Mary Elizabeth Combe in the mid 1960s, who lovingly converted the house to a restaurant when it became Pierre's, owned by Pierre Cassan. Later, it was Jimmy's French Restaurant, owned by Jimmy Rallis.

Richard and Kathy Whisenhunt bought the business and brought it to new life as *The Black Swan*. The Whisenhunts have put their own signature on the restaurant's cuisine and decor, and have added the perennial and vegetable gardens in the back.

This is your opportunity to host a larger dinner party as *The Black Swan* recipes included serve eight people.

The Black Swan, Historic Route 7A,
Manchester, Vermont 05254 (802) 362-3807

1. Grilled Swordfish
With Cilantro Salsa

On The Menu *(Service For Eight)*

Shrimp And Corn Fritters
Grilled Endive And Radiccio Salad
Grilled Fresh Swordfish With Cilantro Salsa Over Black Bean Chili
Coffee Toffee Pie

Shrimp And Corn Fritters

1½ cups flour
2 tsps baking powder
1 tsp salt
1 pinch black pepper *(ground)*
½ cup chives *(diced)*
1 large egg
½ cup milk
1 tbls clarified butter
1½ cups corn kernals
½ cup shrimp *(diced)*

Combine dry ingredients in large mixing bowl. Add corn and shrimp and mix well. Combine egg, milk and butter in a separate bowl, and mix well. Add milk mixture to dry ingredients and mix thoroughly. Drop tablespoons of batter into hot oil and deep fry until golden brown. Serve hot, napped with Saffron Cream Sauce.

Saffron Cream Sauce:
3 cups champagne
2 cups heavy cream
½ tsp saffron
salt and pepper to taste

In a sauce pan, reduce champagne by ¾; add cream and saffron and slowly reduce until sauce begins to thicken. Add salt and pepper to taste.

Grilled Endive And Radiccio Salad

4 heads endive *(½ head per person)*
2 heads radiccio

For each salad: Cut endive in half length-wise. Place on hot grill and press to fan out leaves. Grill 2-3 minutes and turn over and grill another 2-3 minutes. Place ½ endive on a bed of radiccio leaves *(about ¼ head per person)* and drizzle Shallot Vinaigrette.

Shallot Vinaigrette:
1 egg
¼ cup shallots *(finely diced)*
½ cup sherry vinegar
½ tsp salt
2 tbls parsley *(chopped)*
3½ cups soybean oil
½ cup water

Mix together egg, shallots, vinegar, salt and parsley. Put into food processor and slowly add oil and water until blended and smooth. Can be whisked together if you do not have a food processor.

Grilled Fresh Swordfish With Cilantro Salsa Over Black Bean Chili

Grill one 8 oz fresh swordfish steak per person over coals for 2-3 minutes on each side. Serve on a bed of black bean chili, topped with a generous serving of cilantro salsa, garnished with several tortilla chips.

Black Bean Chili:
2 cups dried black beans
1 large onion *(diced)*
8 cups water
2 tbls cumin
2 tbls garlic *(diced)*
1 cup tomato *(diced)*
2 tsp oregano
1 tsp black pepper
1 bay leaf

Soak beans overnight in water. In large sauce pan, lightly sauté onions in oil until soft. Drain beans and rinse; add to onions. Add the rest of the ingredients, including water, and cook at a slow boil until mixture reaches a thick paste consistency *(add more water if necessary).* Add salt and cumin to taste.

Cilantro Salsa:
4 large tomatoes *(diced)*
1 medium red onion *(diced)*
1 bunch scallions
3 tbls cilantro *(chopped)*
½ tsp cumin
salt and pepper

Mix diced tomatoes, onions, scallions together; add cilantro and cumin. Salt and pepper to taste. Chill.

Coffee Toffee Pie

Filling:
½ lb soft sweet butter
1 cup brown sugar
4 tsp instant coffee
2 tsp vanilla
3 oz semi-sweet chocolate *(melted)*
4 eggs

Topping:
2 cups heavy cream *(very cold)*
2 tbls + 1 tsp instant coffee
½ cup powdered sugar
2 tbls unsweetened cocoa
1 tsp vanilla
2 tbls chocolate (finely ground)

Filling: In mixer, cream butter until fluffy and smooth, add the sugar, coffee, and vanilla and beat until smooth. Next add the melted chocolate, again beat until smooth. Add eggs one by one, beating for several minutes after each addition. Spread the mixture into the pie shell. Chill several hours. *(At this point, the pies can be wrapped and frozen.)*

Make the topping 2-3 hours before serving: Whip together the cream, coffee, powdered sugar, cocoa, and vanilla until very stiff. Spoon into pastry bag with a large star tip and cover top of pie in large rosettes. Garnish top with grated chocolate. *(An important note: Always keep refrigerated.)*

Crust:
1 cup flour
¼ tsp salt
1/3 cup brown sugar
1/3 cup butter *(cold)*
3 tbls chocolate *(finely chopped)*
¾ cup walnuts *(chopped)*
1 tsp vanilla
2 tsp water

Combine the flour, salt, and brown sugar. With a pastry blender cut in the butter. Stir in the chocolate and nuts. Mix the vanilla and water and add to the flour mixture. Work mixture with your hands to combine. With floured hands, push the mixture into a 9-inch pie shell covering bottom, sides, and rim. Bake for 20 minutes at 350 degrees. Remove and cool completely.

Wine Suggestions

Graves, Chateau de Chantegrieve; Chardonnay, Edna Valley; Quady Orange Muscat.

2. Fricassee Of Chicken At The Black Swan

On The Menu: (Service For Eight)

Fresh Maine Crab Cakes; Roasted Red Pepper Coulis
Mesclun Greens with Tahini Vinaigrette
Fricassee of Chicken with Calimyrna Figs and Mushrooms
Baked Mascarpone Cheese with Fresh Fruit

Fresh Maine Crab Cakes With Roasted Red Pepper Coulis

2 lbs crab meat
2 cups mayonnaise
1 cup dijon mustard *(spicy)*
1 tbls Worcestershire sauce
1 tsp Tabasco
½ cup chives *(chopped)*
4 eggs
1½ cups bread crumbs

In bowl, mix mayonnaise, mustard, eggs, Worcestershire sauce, tabasco, and chives together until smooth. Add crab meat and mix completely. Slowly add ¾ of the bread crumbs, let rest 5 minutes. If mixture is still wet, add rest of bread crumbs. When shaping, use ice cream scoop to portion, Lightly dust with bread crumbs. Sauté in oil about 3 minutes on each side. Nap with roasted red pepper coulis.

Roasted Red Pepper Coulis:
2 cups champagne
1 cup heavy cream
2 red peppers
salt and white pepper

Place whole peppers under broiler until skin begins to blister and turn black. Rotate pepper until the whole pepper is blistered. Place in ice water for about 10 minutes. Skin should peel off easily. Remove skins, seeds and stems and discard.

In a non-aluminum saucepan over medium high heat, reduce the champagne by ¾. Add peppers and cream and cook slowly until sauce begins to thicken. Remove from heat and place mixture in blender and blend until smooth. Salt and pepper to taste. Can be served hot or cold.

Greens With Tahini Vinaigrette

1 cup orange juice concentrate
2 eggs
½ cup rice wine vinegar

1 cup sesame tahini
¼ cup soy sauce
2 tbls Worcestershire sauce
3 cups olive oil

In a food processor place eggs, orange juice and vinegar; mix until smooth. Turn machine off. Add tahini, soy sauce, Worcestershire sauce and tabasco. Mix again for about a minute. With machine running, slowly add oil. If dressing is too thin, add more oil. If too thick, add small amount of water. Dressing will keep refrigerated for about 2 weeks. Toss with mesclun greens.

Fricassee of Chicken With Calmyrna Figs And Mushrooms

4 tbls cooking oil
4 lbs skinless, boneless chicken meat *(cut into medium pieces)*
2 lbs medium mushrooms *(stemmed and cut)*
1 lb dried figs *(halved)*
½ cup sweet Marsala wine
4 cups chicken stock
1 cup Dijon mustard
2 tbls brown sugar
salt and pepper

In a large sauté pan, heat oil until very hot, place chicken in pan and sauté until brown. Remove from pan and set aside. Sauté mushrooms and figs in same pan for 2-3 minutes; deglaze pan with Marsala and add chicken stock to mushroom-fig mixture. Add brown sugar and mustard to mixture and bring to a slow boil. Add chicken pieces and reduce sauce until mixture begins to thicken. Salt and pepper to taste. Serve with new potatoes.

Baked Mascarpone Cheese With Fruit

32 oz Mascarpone cheese
2 cups brown sugar
1½ cups walnuts *(chopped)*
Fresh strawberries *(whole)* or apples *(sliced)*

In individual ovenproof dishes, spoon in 3-4 oz Mascarpone Cheese. On top of cheese, firmly pack about ½ inch of brown sugar. On top of that, place a layer of chopped walnuts. Bake in 375 degree oven for 5 minutes. Serve with your favorite fresh fruit for dipping.

Wine Suggestions

Georges duBoeuf Macon Villages; Chardonnay, Chateau St. Jean Robert Young Vineyard; Warre's Late Bottled Vintage Port

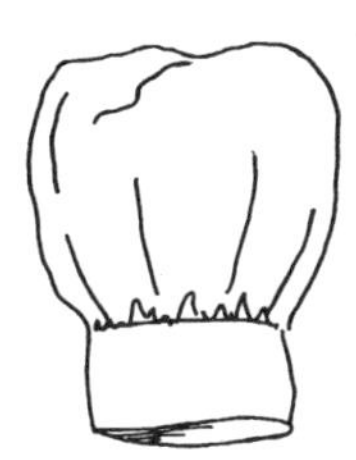

Meet The Black Swan Chef Richard Whisenhunt

Chef Whisenhunt of *The Black Swan*, born and raised in Marin County, California, began his culinary career in Sausalito at The Alta Mira Hotel. He moved on to Ondine's and Le Club on Nob Hill in San Francisco. He came east to New York City in 1979 to become an apprentice at the 3-star Le Cirque for two years, working every station from butchering to baking.

After a honeymoon/culinary tour of France in 1981, Richard and his wife Kathy moved back to Marin County just as California cuisine was changing everyone's outlook on the food and restaurant industry. He became head chef at a small Chez Panisse-style restaurant in San Rafael where he began to experiment with new tastes and cooking styles. All the while, he used his classical French training as a solid base for this experimentation. The result is his own eclectic style of cooking.

Richard and Kathy decided to venture out on their own after four years to seek a place that fit their own personalities and talents. After scouring California to no avail, they took some advice of friends and visited Manchester, and after just four days they knew they would find a home here.

While waiting for the right restaurant to become available in the Northshire, the Whisenhunts spent a year in Greenwich, Connecticut where he was the Sous Chef at The Homestead Inn.

Soon, Jimmy's came on the market and on December 27, 1985, *The Black Swan* was accepted onto the burgeoning Manchester scene. Just 10 days later, the couple welcomed son Josh into the world.

Over the next several years, Richard and Kathy redecorated the interior, added a dining room and cocktail lounge, landscaped perennial flower gardens in the back yard and a vegetable garden for fresh herbs and vegetables.

Come meet the Whisenhunts at *The Black Swan*. Richard oversees the kitchen production and Kathy will greet you at the door.

The Equinox Hotel & Resort

Of History And Grandeur In Manchester Village

The stately *Equinox Hotel and Resort* spans 1,100 acres nestled between the Green and Taconic Mountain ranges at the base of 3,800 foot Mt. Equinox and is the centerpiece of Manchester Village. The resort includes the historic Equinox Hotel with 136 rooms in its main building and 27 in adjacent townhouses, fitness spa and the *Gleneagles Golf Course at The Equinox,* an 18-hole championship-quality golf course and clubhouse, Equinox Hotel and part of Mt. Equinox itself.

The famous resort was purchased by Equinox Resort Associates, a partnership established by Guinness Enterprise Holdings (Vermont), Callaghan & Partners, Ltd. and The Galesi Group with one goal in mind:"To establish The Equinox as the premier destination resort in the Northeast." The unique property has been completely revitalized.

A sense of history is everywhere. And, why not? It all began in 1769 when the stoic, two-story wooden lodging, The Marsh Tavern, was founded on its site. The tavern would become an important meeting place for American Revolutionaries, including the legendary Green Mountain Boys. It is also significant as the first Tory (British loyalist) property seized by revolutionaries to support their war efforts. Thaddeus Munson expanded the territory of the tavern by adding a new inn next door; more than a one-half dozen of the subsequent owners did likewise over two centuries.

The hotel received its present name in 1849 when Franklin Orvis began taking in summer guests at the hotel in the house his father built next to the tavern. Its reputation as a premiere summer resort was cemented in 1863 when Mrs. Abraham Lincoln visited with her two sons. The hotel has also hosted Ulysses S. Grant and Teddy Roosevelt.

Mountain Stirrings features two complete dinners by Executive Chef Brian Aspell; one is from the grand *Colonnade,* which offers an elegant dining experience featuring fine cuisine and wines, and the other from the *Marsh Tavern*, the authentic showplace of the hotel.

The Equinox Hotel and Resort, Historic Route 7A South,
Manchester Village, Vermont 05254. (802) 362-4700, (800) 362-4747

---

1. A Grand Dinner From The Colonnade

On The Menu:

Mascarpone Basil Torta With Smoked Tomato Vinaigrette
Wild Mushroom Cream With Hickory Partridge And Bacon
Roasted Loin of Vermont VenisonWith Grilled Ratatouille And Semolina
Hazlenut Hippen With Vermont Blueberries And Warm Sabayon

Mascarpone Basil TortaWith Smoked Tomato Vinaigrette

1 tsp butter *(room temperature)*
¼ cup Ritz cracker crumbs
½ cup Asiago cheese *(grated)*
16 oz. Mascarpone
10 whole eggs, 4 yolks
¼ cup pine nuts *(baked, crushed)*
½ cup basil pesto
cayenne pepper *(to taste)*
salt
fresh basil leaves

Coat a 2 inch deep baking pan with butter. Mix Ritz cracker crumbs and asiago together and then apply to baking pan to form a crust.

Mix Mascarpone and the remaining ingredients in a mixing bowl until you have attained a smooth pale green batter. Pour into baking pan and bake at 350 degrees for 40 minutes or until a golden crust has formed. Make certain to rotate the pan while baking in order to ensure an even color. Five minutes before removing from the oven, sprinkle a thin layer of the crushed pine nuts, forming an even crust.

Once cool, cut into desired shape and place on a sheet pan for reheating. The fresh basil leaves will serve as a garnish for service. Just prior to service, reheat the portions in a 350 degree oven. Serving this dish warm enhances the mascarpone greatly.

Smoked Tomato Vinaigrette

¼ cup shallots *(roasted)*
1 tbls capers
3 cloves garlic *(roasted)*
5, 5"x6" beef steak tomatoes *(split, seeded and smoked)*
½ cup balsamic vinegar
1 tsp.salt
1 tsp. dry mustard
1 tbls olive oil
1 cup white wine

Smoke the tomatoes, cover and allow to sit overnight in the refrigerator.

Roast garlic and shallots separately until golden in color. Deglase the garlic, add shallots and reduce the white wine by half its volume, cool and chop into a fine paste. In a food processor, purée the tomato, add the garlic and shallots followed by the remainder of the ingredients and purée further. Strain and cool for service. If necessary, adjust the seasoning with some salt and white pepper.

When presenting the dish, place 3 large circles of the vinaigrette on a plate, drizzle some extra virgin olive oil randomly over the vinaigrette. Around the perimeter of the plate, sprinkle some fresh cracked black pepper and shaved Asiago cheese. Set the re-heated (warm) torta in the center of the plate, garnish with the fresh basil.

I suggest contacting *Vermont Butter and Cheese* in Websterville at (802) 479-9371 for their Mascarpone and other high quality dairy products.

Wild Mushroom Cream With Hickory Partridge And Bacon

6, 16 oz avg Partridges *(breast meat removed)*
2 quart chicken stock
1 onion *(chopped)*
2 celery stalks *(chopped)*
2 carrots *(chopped)*
2 sprigs fresh thyme

Remove the breast meat and any skin left on the birds. Roast in 350 degree oven until birds are golden in color. Place the birds in a stock pot with the chicken stock, parsely and vegetables. Rreduce for 40 minutes, strain and hold for soup.

6-8 oz leeks *(rinsed and chopped)*
6 shallots *(peeled and chopped)*
1½ pound wild mushrooms *(Note: If necessary, a good assortment of wild mushrooms can be purchased dry. Look for a mix of cepes, porcini morel mushrooms.)*
2 quarts partridge stock
Sachet bag, fresh thyme, bay leaf, peppercorns
¼ lb butter
½ cup flour
2 Russet potatoes *(peeled, diced)*
1 cup dry white wine
½ cup dry sherry
¼ lb maple or honey cured bacon

Melt butter and add leeks, shallots, sachet and potatoes. Allow this to cook for several minutes and then add mushrooms. Cook several minutes and gradually add flour. When flour is blended, add white wine, reduce by half the wine's volume and then add partridge stock. Once soup simmers, stir to dissove all the flour. Simmer for 15 minutes, remove the sachet bag and puree the soup. Adjust the seasoning with salt and pepper and hold warm for service.

With some hickory chips, lightly smoke the partridge breasts, then roast them in a 350 degree oven for 30 minutes. Once cooled, cut into match size *(julienne)* and use to garnish the soup.

Bacon:

Cut raw bacon into Julienne strips (*this is easier and safer if bacon is frozen).* Cook the cut bacon in a pan until crisp, drain well and sprinkle on soup for garnish.If you prefer, some heavy cream may be used to finish the soup. I suggest contacting Bill and Rick Thompson at *Cavendish Game Birds* at (802) 885-1183.

Roasted Loin of Vermont Venison

Plan on about 4-6 oz. of venison per guest. You will need that weight for this recipe to come from either the loin or rib section. The cut should be boneless.

32 oz venison *(rib or loin, cut into 6 inch medallions)*
salt, cracked black pepper
olive oil

Place some olive oil in a skillet, heat and sear the venison. Before searing the meat, season with salt and black pepper. Once seared, allow to cool.

½ cup whole grain mustard
1 tbls rosemary *(chopped)*
¼ cup chopped parsley *(chopped)*
2 cups fresh bread crumbs
salt, pepper *(to taste)*

Brush the venison with the mustard. Make a bread crumb mixture with the remaining ingredients. Dredge the venison in that mixture and finish cooking in the oven at 350 degrees until an internal temperature of 140 degrees is achieved. This should take about 30 minutes. Remove venison from oven and hold warm for service.

1 box cous cous
chicken stock
¼ lb. Asiago cheese *(shredded)*

Cook the cous cous. When finished, stir in the shredded cheese and place on a 1-inch deep cookie pan. Place in freezer to chill. Once cool, use a cookie cutter and cut out circles, 4 inches in diameter. When the lamb has finished, these cous cous cakes will be used under the sliced lamb. Slightly sauté cakes to reheat.

½ cup olive oil
1 bulb fennel
1 zuccini
1 yellow squash
1 ea. yellow, red, green bell peppers
1 med. eggplant
1 Spanish onion
2 tomatoes *(large)*
1 bunch basil *(chopped)*
salt, pepper *(to taste)*
1 tbls garlic, *chopped*

Rinse and split all of the vegetables and place them on the charbroiler for several seconds *(enough time to pick up grill marks)*. Once all vegetables are cool, cut them into a small dice. In a pan, sauté the garlic in olive oil. Add the remaining vegetables and sauté until tender. Season with salt and pepper.

For service, place a reheated cous cous circle in the center of a plate. Carefully place a 1 inch layer of ratatouille on the cous cous cakes. Slice the venison into ¼ inch thick slices and arrange attractively atop the ratatouille. The dish can be garnished with some fresh rosemary, basil or other fresh herbs.

For fresh Vermont venison, contact Joe Delfino at *Old Moses Farm* in Strafford (802) 765-4645.

Hazlenut Hippen With Vermont Berries And Warm Sabayon

5 cups Vermont berries *(strawberries, blackberries, blueberries)*
½ cup Grand Marnier
½ cup Cassis Liqueur
To Taste: 10X sugar

Trim, rinse and drain the berries. Dissolve the 10X sugar in a bowl, combining the 2 liquors. Delicately toss the berries in the liqueur/sugar mixture and refrigerate.

Hippen Cups:
15 oz almond paste
4 oz praline paste
11 oz 10x sugar
1 pt egg whites
½ pt heavy cream
6 oz bread flour

Cream almond paste, praline paste and sugar together until smooth. Scrape down sides of bowl, add whites very slowly while mixing on second speed, scrapping down sides occasionally. When smooth, add cream and flour, mix until incorporated.

Spread 6 inch circles of batter on greased sheetpan and bake at 350 degrees for 6-8 minutes *(until slightly golden in color).* While still warm, lift the baked batter circles off with a spatula and use a soup cup to form the rounds into a soup cup shape. This will be used to present the berries.

For the Sabayon:
¼ cup orange juice
¼ cup Madiera wine
¼ cup Cassis
¼ cup Goldschlager
½ cup brown sugar *(granulated)*
10 ea egg yolks
Vanilla extract *(to taste)*

Place ingredients into 2-quart stainless steel bowl. Whisk over a double boiler until ribbons appear and a thick, creamy consistency is achieved.

Fill the hippen cups with berries and some of the liqueur/sugar mixture. Just before serving, place a ribbon of warm sabayon over the berries and garnish with some fresh mint. For some of the most flavorfull berries, visit the *Smokey House Project* in Danby, (802), 293-5121..This is a non-profit program, producing high quality crops.

Wine Suggestion

Since all of our menus in both the Colonnade and Marsh Tavern reflect regional New England foods, it is appropriate we pair these menus with a well balanced wine from the Northeast.

The soil conditions of Southeastern New England closely resemble the composition of some of the Northern European wine producing areas. Combined with the proximity to the Atlantic make the region conducive to an even growing, ripening season.

Sakonnet Vineyards, (401) 635-8486, located in Little Compton, Rhode Island, is on 44 acres of this prime New England soil and has a wonderful selection of wines, some of which have received national notoriety.

For this menu: *Sakonnet America's Cup White for appetizer; Sakonnet Barrel Select Pinot Noir for entree.*

2. Authentic New England Dining From The Marsh Tavern

On The Menu

Guinness Stout and Cheddar Chowder With Anadama Bread
Strudel of Summertime Chanterelles With Sage And Plum Tomatoes
Apple Roasted Pheasant With Potato, Bacon And Onion Cake And Cider Jus
Warm Banana Betty With Gingersnap Crumbs

Guinness Stout and Cheddar Chowder with Anadama Bread

4 oz onions
4 oz leeks
1 oz shallots
4 oz butter
4 oz AP flour
½ gal flavorful chicken stock
1 lb Grafton cheddar *(grated)*
4 oz Guinness Stout
1 cup heavy cream
2 tsp whole grain mustard
Tabasco sauce *(to taste)*
2 oz ea red, green, yellow bell peppers
2 oz chives
Sachet bag
salt, white pepper

In a soup pot, sauté the onions, leeks, shallots and butter until translucent. Add the flour to create a roux and cook for 3 minutes stirring frequently. Add chicken stock and sachet bag. Allow to simmer for 15 minutes. Strain out the cooked vegetables and sachet bag, return the soup to a simmer. Stir in grated cheddar and add mustard, stout and cream. Stir frequently until all cheddar melts. Cut pepper and chives into a fine dice and blanch by sautéing them quickly. Add the pepper and chives to the soup, season with tabasco, salt and white pepper. I recommend *Grafton Village Premium Cheddar,* a very flavorful and unique cheddar selection, for this recipe.

Anadama Bread:

Legend has it that a woman named Anna put too much flour in her cornbread and her husband exclaimed, *"Anna, Damn Her!."* Makes 5, ½ pound loaves.

3/8 cup corn meal
1¾ cup water
3/8 cup dark molasses

1½ tbls shortening
2 tsp dry yeast
1 3/4 cup water
4½ cups bread flour *(amount of flour varies...just ask Anna!)*
1 tsp salt

Bring water, molasses and shortening to a boil first. Whisk in cornmeal. Cook until thick, allow to cool. Bloom yeast in second water *(make sure it is warm).* Kneed together all ingredients until elastic. Allow to rise 1 hour, cut into loaves and allow to rise 1 hour. Bake at 350 degrees and garnish top with cornmeal.

Strudel Of Summertime Chanterelles With Sage And Plum Tomatoes

2 lbs fresh Chanterelle mushrooms *(quartered)*
½ lb fresh Cremini mushrooms *(quartered)*
6 ea shallots *(chopped fine)*
1 tsp fresh thyme *(chopped fine)*
¼ lb butter
5 sheets phyllo dough
¼ lb butter
bread crumbs
½ cup dry white wine
6 ea plum tomatoes *(large dice, and seeded)*
2 tsp fresh sage *(chopped fine)*
2 ea scallions *(chopped fine)*
2 ea shallots *(chopped fine)*
1 pinch cracked white pepper
¼ cup dry white wine
2 whole eggs
salt *(to taste)*

In a sauté pan melt ¼ lb butter and add shallots, sauté slightly. Add the mushrooms, sauté slightly. Add ½ cup dry white wine, allow wine to simmer and reduce. When wine is reduced by half, stir in scallions, thyme, white pepper and reduce until mixture is moist *(not dry).* Cool to room temperature and stir in eggs.

Place a layer of phyllo dough on clean, dry work space and brush on a layer of butter. Dust with bread crumbs and repeat atop the previous sheet with the remaining 4 phyllo sheets. Place the abovemushroom mixture along the long end of the phyllo dough. Carefully roll into a fairly tight strudel.

Place this strudel in a 350 degree oven and bake until phyllo begins to turn yellow in color. Remove from oven and allow to partially cool for slicing.

While strudel is baking, place butter in a sauté pan with shallots, scallions, sage and white pepper. Sauté briefly and add the plum tomatoes. Sauté briefly and add the white wine. Reduce the white wine until it is almost dry and season if necessary with salt. Place a ladle of this tomato, sage ragout on a plate. Set a slice of strudel and garnish with some fresh sage leaves.

I suggest foraging on *Mount Equinox* for finding the freshest chanterelles. If that doesn't appeal to you, contact *Black River Produce* of Proctor, (802) 336-7484, a good source for truly Vermont specialties such as chanterelles, fiddleheads and chestnuts. Ned Swansberg of the *Vermont Institute of National Science* in Manchester conducts very informative hikes devoted to the search for wild edibles.

Apple Roasted Pheasant
With Potato, Onion and Bacon Cake -- Cider Jus

3, 2¼ lb pheasants
2 Cortland apples *(sliced)*
2 onions *(sliced)*
1 stalk carrot
1 stalk celery
salt and pepper

In a hot sauté pan, quickly toss the apples and onions until they are golden in color. Use these onions and apples as stuffing to place inside the pheasant before roasting. Season inside and outside of pheasant with salt and pepper.

Roast the pheasants in a 350 degree oven until they are 75 percent cooked. Remove from roasting pan and cool. When cool enough to handle, split and remove the rib bones. Also remove last leg section from thigh. Set thigh and some boneless breast aside.

Place pheasant necks, bones and last leg sections in roasting pan and roast until evenly brown. Add apple/onion mixture with 1 stalk of carrot and celery to the bones and continue to roast for 10 minutes.

Cider jus:
1 quart chicken stock
1 sprig fresh thyme
4 bay leaves
pinch peppercorns
1 tsp tomato paste
1 cup apple cider
arrowroot

Place tomato paste in the above roasting pan and roast in oven for several minutes. Remove the roasting pan from oven and place on stove top. Add chicken stock, cider, thyme, bay leaf and peppercorns and reduce by half. Thicken with mixture of chicken stock and arrowroot and strain.

Place pheasant breast and thigh in oven and finish roasting. For service, place pheasant on the potato cake. Garnish the cider jus with some Julienne green and red apples and nape the pheasant with jus. You may enhance the dish further with native, seasonal vegetables. I recommend contacting Matt and Scout Proft of East Dorset's *Someday Farm,* (802) 362-2290. The Proft's hand feed the finest pheasants I've seen and have a wonderful selection of organic vegetables.

Potato, Onion and Bacon Cake:
2½ lb Yukon Gold potatoes *(peeled, grated, drained well)*
1 lb onions *(grated)*
4 eggs
1 tsp potato starch
1 oz Matzo Meal
salt and pepper *(to taste)*
¼ lb bacon *(diced and cooked)*

Place grated potatoes in a strainer and remove as much liquid as possible. Combine grated onions, potatoes, eggs, potato starch, matzo meal, bacon and season with salt and pepper. Place a 4-inch circular cutter in an oiled non-stick frying pan and place 1 inch of the potato mixture into the cookie cutter. Sauté until golden in color and flip carefully. Remove from pan when golden.

Warm Banana Betty

4 bananas *(peeled and sliced)*
Custard:
2 cups milk
4 oz sugar
1 egg
1 oz cornstarch
2 tsp butter
vanilla to taste

Heat milk and ½ the sugar in saucepan over medium heat.Mix remaining sugar, egg and cornstarch in bowl away from heat. When milk and sugar mixture come to simmer, slowly pour small amount into egg mixture, whisking constantly. Return this to hot milk on stove, cook to pudding stage. Strain into shallow pan and whisk in butter. Cool to room temperature.

Crumb topping:
4 gingersnap cookies
2 graham crackers
1 oz butter *(melted)*

In shallow earthenware baking dishes, ladle in custard mix. Place sliced banana in each, top with crumb mixture and heat in microwave for 2 minutes on high setting.

Wine Suggestion

Sakonnet Estate Bottled Chardonnay with strudel; Sakonnet Estate Bottled Vidal Blanc with entree.

Meet Equinox Hotel Executive Chef Brian Aspell

Brian Aspell uses his diverse experience from some world class resorts to bring out the best of fresh Vermont agriculture in developing the first-class cuisine of *The Equinox.* As Executive Chef, Chef Aspell is responsible for all dining facilities of the resort complex, including the *Marsh Tavern, Colonnade, Dormy Grill* at the Country Club and all catering functions.

Chef Aspell recently helped to organize the successful *"Taste of Vermont"* event with local producers, farmers and chefs to promote regional produce and dining. He is active in the Southern Vermont Community Agricultural Center, a group working collectively with the Vermont Department of Agriculture.

His work has taken him throughout the U.S. and overseas as well. Most recently, he was Executive Chef for Rockresorts in Little Dix Bay, British Virgin Islands. He has served the Williamsburg Inn in Virginia, The Woodstock Inn and Resort in Vermont, The White Elephant on Nantucket Island, Massachusetts and Engels in Rotterdam, the Netherlands.

Chef Aspell studied at the Culinary Institute of America in New York and has received numerous awards and citations including The Société Culinaire Philantropique in 1979 and 1983 Culinary Arts Salon; the Nations Capitol Chefs Association 1979 Culinary Arts Salon; The Tidewater Food Exhibition 1988 Culinary Arts Salon and has attained Certified Executive Chef status with the American Culinary Federation Educational Institute. He is president of the Vermont Chef's Association, a chapter of the American Culinary Federation. Most recently, he was voted a member of The New England Escoffier Society and the North Eastern Chaine de Rotiseur.

The *Colonnade Room* received a 4-diamond award of which Chef Aspell and his staff are extremely proud.

The Equinox Mountain Inn

The Stars Are So Close You Can Touch Them

Dining at the Equinox Mountain Inn means enjoying a different experience in a very special place...on top of Mount Equinox, in the highest range in South western Vermont at 3,835 feet. You're surrounded by 8,000 pristine acres and will dine in an art deco building, circa 1949. It is New England's only full-service mountain top inn and the 360-degree panoramic view takes in Vermont, New York, Massachusetts and Canada.

An inexplicable lure drew the Indians to hunt and forage Ekwanok (place where the top is) rather than the safer, gentler slopes of the surrounding hills. During Revolutionary War times, Vermont's Ethan Allen lived on its eastern slope. Settlers to the north and south built roads between Beartown and Southeast corners, climbing to the peak and carving their initials in stones to prove they succeeded (now incorporated into the hearth). Frank Orvis and a group of Manchester residents built a four-mile wagon road that rose 1,600 vertical feet.

An organic chemist and avid hiker named Dr. J.G. Davidson acquired 8,000 acres in 1939 to protect the area from development and to share it with future generations. Interrupted by World War II, construction on his home, the five-mile toll road, nine-room inn and hyrdroelectric plant that still powers the mountain, were completed in 1948. An 11-room addition was built in 1964. Dr. Davidson entrusted the estate to Carthusian monks upon his death in the mid-1960s. His verbal proviso was that the toll road remain open and the inn leased to an independent innkeeper; a promise honored.

That same indefinable lure brought current Innkeeper Holly Armitage to the mountaintop in 1993. The inn has been completely renovated with a successful effort made to return this seasonal inn to its original ambiance. To withstand the mountaintop ravages of winter, the outside of this one-of-a-kind property was literally built like a fortress. As Holly puts it, "It will never be Newhart, but it stands grandly and securely on its mountain peak."

Join Chefs Daniel Boepple and Mark Schecter for gourmet dining where the sunsets are later, the moon is brighter and the stars are so close you can touch them.

Equinox Mountain Inn, Skyline Drive,
Arlington, Vermont 05250, (803) 362-1113

1. Franciase At The Summit

On The Menu

Baked Artichokes
Garden Salad With Dan's House Dressing
Pork Tenderloins And Crustless Spinach Pie
Carmel Apple Pie

Baked Artichokes

12 ounces canned artichokes *(drained, chopped)*
½ cup mayonnaise
1 tbls scallions *(chopped)*
¾ cup parmesan and romano cheese *(grated)*
2 tbls Marsala wine

Combine all ingredients in food processor. Place in greased baking dish. Bake at 375 degrees for 30 minutes.

Garden Salad With Dan's House Dressing

¾ cup Balsamic vinegar
juice of 1 lemon
3 cloves garlic *(large, crushed)*
¾ cup honey mustard
1/3 cup dill *(tightly packed)*
4½ cups olive oil
½ tsp pepper *(fresh ground)*

Combine vinegar, lemon, garlic, mustard and ½ cup oil in food processor and blend with motor running. Gradually add remaining oil. When incorporated, add dill and pepper and pulse to combine.

Honey Mustard:
1½ cups Coleman's mustard
½ cup sugar
3 eggs
¼ cup honey

Soak mustard in vinegar overnight. Beat eggs. Add sugar, honey and mustard mixture. Cook in double boiler over low heat until mustard thickens to pudding consistency. Stir constantly. Pour into container and refrigerate.

Pork Tenderloins And Crustless Spinach Pie

2½ lbs tenderloins of pork (6-8 oz per person)
3 tbls sage
1 tbls Coleman's mustard
4 cloves garlic

1 tbls orange juice concentrate
½ cup olive oil *(extra virgin)*

Mix with Sweda Wand and rub marinate on prepared pork tenderloins. Cook in 475 degree oven for 12 minutes.

Sauce: (Make ahead)
8 oz marmalade
1 tbls Coleman's mustard
1 oz Triple Sec
1 oz white vinegar
1 tbls brown sugar
Mix with wand. Sizzle in pan before plating.

Crustless Spinach Pie:
½ lb Ricotta cheese
½ cup grated Mozzarella cheese
2 eggs *(slightly beaten)*
5 oz frozen spinach *(thawed and drained)*
1 tbls vegetable oil
1 clove garlic *(crushed)*

Combine cheeses with eggs. Mix well. Blend in spinach. Add remaining ingredients. Pour into buttered 10-inch spring form pan. Drizzle top with oil. Bake in pre-heated 350 degree oven for 40 minutes. Serve warm or at room temperature.

Caramel Apple Pie

Pie crust (for 1, 9-inch pie);

4-6 tart apples *(pared, cored, sliced)*
1/8 cup sugar
1 tbls flour
½ tsp cinnamon
¼ tsp salt
1 tbls butter *(melted)*
1/8 cup corn syrup *(dark)*

Arrange apples in prepared bottom crust. Combine next 6 ingredients and pour over apples. Adjust top crust and seal. Cut slits in top crust to allow steam to escape. Bake for 40 minutes in a 425 degree oven.

Caramel topping:
1/8 cup brown sugar
1 tbls flour
1 tbls butter
¼ cup corn syrup *(dark)*
¼ cup walnuts *(chopped)*

Combine all ingredients except nuts. Remove pie from oven and pour topping over entire top crust. Sprinkle with walnuts. Return pie to oven and bake 5 more minutes or until topping is bubbly and hot. *(A baking sheet under the pie will catch any run-off.)*

Wine Suggestion:
Jadot Pinot Noir

2. Veal & Shrimp At The Mountaintop

On The Menu

Mushrooms Stuffed With Spinach, Onions And Garlic
Caesar Salad
Veal And Shrimp Francaise With Honeyed Carrots And Broccoli
Caribbean Bananas Flambé

Mushrooms Stuffed With Spinach, Onions And Garlic

1 lb large mushroom caps *(3 per person)*
1 pkg. spinach *(frozen, chopped fine)*
1 large onion *(diced)*
2 large garlic cloves *(diced)*
black pepper *(to taste)*
1 tsp basil *(to taste)*
Parmesan cheese *(to sprinkle)*
wedges of 2 lemons *(dipped in paprika)*

Thaw frozen chopped spinach and drain all water. Chop fine and sauté diced onions and garlic. Add spinach and season with black pepper and basil. Sauté until onions are transparent *(about 5 minutes)*. Stuff into large mushroom caps.

Marinara sauce:
1 clove garlic *(minced)*
2 tbls olive oil
2½ cups Italian tomatoes *(drained)*
½ tsp oregano
1 tbls parsley *(chopped)*

Sauté garlic in olive oil and add remainder of ingredients. Bring to a boil. Reduce heat and simmer uncovered for 15-20 minutes. Cover bottom of casserole with Marinara sauce. Place stuffed mushroom caps on sauce and sprinkle parmesan cheese over it. Bake in 400 degree oven for 10-15 minutes. Serve with 2 lemon wedges.

Caesar Salad

1, 8 oz can anchovies
1 clove garlic *(crushed)*
2 cups virgin olive oil
¼ cup lemon juice
2 tbls Worchestershire sauce
1 egg
1/3 cup parmesan *(grated)*
2 heads Romaine lettuce
garlic croutons

Mash anchovies. Add in olive oil, lemon juice, Worchestershire sauce, egg and parmesan cheese. Blend well and set aside. Rub garlic in wooden bowl. Pare lettuce into bite-sized pieces and place in bowl. Toss with ½ cup dressing *(or more, to taste)*. Top with garlic croutons. Serve chilled on dinner plate. *(Serves six.)*

Veal And Shrimp Francaise With Honeyed Carrots And Broccoli

2½ lbs veal medallions *(7 oz per person)*
12-15 large shrimp *(peeled and de-veined)*
1/8 cup flour
1/8 cup butter
½ cup chicken stock
2 tsp lemon juice
black pepper *(to taste)*
2 eggs
2 tbls olive oil
½ cup white wine *(dry)*

Dredge veal medallions and shrimp in floured egg wash. Sauté in hot oil until lightly brown. Remove from pan. Place on hot serving dish and set aside. Pour out excess oil from pan. Pour in wine to deglaze pan. Add light roux *(butter and flour)* to chicken stock, lemon juice and black pepper. Simmer in pan, stirring constantly. To serve, divide the veal and shrimp onto individual plates and pour sauce over each. *(Serves six.)*

Honeyed Carrots And Broccoli:
1 lb carrots *(sliced)*
1 lb broccoli (florettes)
2 tsp clarified butter
2 tsp honey
1 tsp oregano
black pepper *(to taste)*

Slice carrots into 1/8 inch pieces. Par boil carrots and broccoli about 7 minutes. In sauté pan, add butter, honey, oregano and black pepper. Add carrots and broccoli to pan. Sauté 5 minutes. Serve hot.

Caribbean Bananas Flambé

6 bananas
1 tbls butter
1 tsp nutmeg
brown sugar *(for sprinkling)*
1 oz 150 proof rum
½ tsp lime juice

Slice bananas in half. Simmer in butter and nutmeg until brown on each side. Remove bananas and place into flame-proof pan *(copper is best)*. Sprinkle bananas with brown sugar and lime juice. Pour warmed *(but not boiling)* rum over the top and touch the edge of pan with match *(be careful)*. Let burn out. Divide into 6 servings and serve warm from pan.

Wine Suggestion

Chateau Souverain Chardonnay

Meet Equinox Mountain Inn Chefs Daniel Boepple And Mark Schechter

Working high atop the mountain are two fine chefs. Daniel Boepple is a native of Bennington. He worked in kitchens during high school which earned him the honor of managing the company Bar during his stint in Viet Nam. After his service career, Dan worked for City University Graduate Dining Commons under the tutelage of Chef Mate Clarion (formerly of Demonicos) and Chef Roger France (retired from Four Seasons).

Dan returned to the Brasserie Restaurant in Bennington. Merging his cooking career with another vocation, he then attended the University of Vermont, receiving a degree in Technical Theatre. For the next seven years, he and his wife, Beth, spent winters with the Indiana Repertory Theatre and summers on Cape Cod with the Monomy Theatre, where he was also the company chef. Dan and Beth opened The Villager Restaurant in Bennington.

When Innkeeper Holly Armitage decided to lease the *Equinox Mountain Inn*, it fit Dan and Beth's schedule (she planned to attend Vermont Law School) and it worked out well for everyone. Dan is well-known for his Veal Sweetbreads.

Chef Schechter is a Baltimore native and worked in his family's fish business for a decade before heading for Florida and the hotel business. He worked his way from bellhop to food and beverage manager.

For the next 15 years, Mark managed country clubs in Long Island, Connecticut and New Jersey. He opened his own seafood restaurant at the marina in Clinton, Connecticut and was chef until he took early retirement.

He has been living in the Caribbean on an Island Trader motor sailor, teaching cooking in Grenada (post invasion) and cruising the blue waters. Mark met Holly in St. Thomas in 1987 and responded to her call to Vermont and the *Equinox Mountain Inn.*

The Highland House

150 Years Of Vermont Tradition

The Highland House was originally built in 1842 as a private dwelling, and has welcomed guests and visitors for more than 150 years. Set on 32 acres of scenic countryside and surrounded by stately century-old maples, the 17-room inn offers relaxed and enjoyable hospitality.

The Main House served as a bed and breakfast and apartment before returning to its present role as an inn in 1976. All the rooms in the main house are tastefully decorated with antiques acquired through the years. Guests enjoy sipping iced tea while relaxing in rocking chairs on the front porch during the summer and relax around the cozy wood stove in the winter.

The Waite House, named for Charles Waite the original owner, sits to the rear of the Main House and overlooks the swimming pool. Four of the eight rooms are spacious suites with private sitting areas.

The Green Mountains provide a wonderful backdrop of activities for guests and its location offers ideal access to hiking, swimming, tennis, alpine and cross-country skiing, canoeing, fishing and more. For other diversions, the Weston Playhouse features fine theater attractions and The Weston Priory, a Benedictine monastery, is a short drive away.

The Highland House is proud of its exceptional cuisine, created by Chef Elise Durr, and you'll enjoy the dinners described in our book.

The Highland House, Route 100,
Londonderry, Vermont 05148, (802) 824-3019

1. A Black Tiger Shrimp Dinner

On The Menu

Cutlass Potato Soup
Sweet Poppy Seed Salad
Oriental Black Tiger Shrimp
Frozen Lemon Torte

Cutlass Potato Soup

5 bacon slices
2 tbls (¼ stick) butter
3 medium-large boiling potatoes *(peeled and chopped)*
1 large carrot *(chopped)*
½ medium onion *(chopped)*
3 cups water
2 tsp salt
1/8 tsp pepper *(freshly ground)*
2 cups milk

Fry bacon in heavy large saucepan over medium high heat until crisp. Remove with slotted spoon; drain on paper towels. Crumble bacon and set aside. Pour off drippings. Melt butter in same pan over medium heat. Add vegetables and cook until slightly softened, stirring occasionally, about 15 minutes. Add bacon, water, salt, and pepper. Cover and simmer about 20 minutes until vegetables are tender. Add milk and heat through. Purée slightly until soup thickens. Serve hot.

Sweet Poppy Seed Salad

1½ cups sugar
2 tsp dry mustard
2 tsp salt
2/3 cup vinegar
3 tbls onion juice
2 cups salad oil *(not olive oil)*
3 tbls poppy seeds

Mix all ingredients and blend well in a blender. Add to a mixture of green and red lettuce with shredded carrots, shredded red cabbage, sliced tomato and sliced cucumber.

Oriental Black Tiger Shrimp

20-24 large Black Tiger Shrimp
6 scallions *(chopped)*
3 tbls soy sauce
2 tbls white wine vinegar
2 tbls garlic *(minced)*
2 tbls ginger root *(finely grated)*

4 tsp oriental sesame oil
2 tsp sugar
1 tsp red pepper flakes
½ tsp salt

Peel and de-vein shrimp. Combine all above ingredients and marinate shrimp in mixture for 15 minutes at room temperature. Take shrimp out of mixture and sauté slowly in several tbls of sesame oil. Once shrimp is cooked, remove from pan and place on a bed of rice. Garnish with chopped up scallions. Serve with steamed snow pea pods.

Frozen Lemon Torte

Crust:
1, 5½ pack lemon crunch cookies *(finely crushed)*
6 tbls (¾ stick) butter *(melted)*

Combine crushed cookies and butter and blend well. Pat into bottom of spring form pan. Refrigerate.

Lemon filling:
4 egg whites
1 cup sugar
4 egg yolks
½ cup lemon juice
1½ tbls lemon peel
1½ cups whipping cream

Beat egg whites on medium speed until foamy. Gradually add sugar, beating until stiff peaks form. Beat yolks in another bowl until thick and lemon colored. Stir in lemon juice and lemon peel. Gently fold egg whites into yolks. Fold cream into mixture. Pour into pan and freeze for 8 hours.

Purée raspberries with some sugar and pour a bit of the mixture over each serving of torte.

Wine Suggestion

Chardonnay, Chateau Montelena

2. Dining With A Drunken Chicken

On The Menu

Carrot Vichyssoise
Raspberry Vinaigrette Salad
Drunken Chicken With Fresh Steamed Broccoli And Rosemary Roasted Potaotes
Apple Crisp

Carrot Vichyssoise

1½ cups potatoes *(peeled, diced)*
1¼ cups carrots *(sliced)*
1 leek *(sliced, white part)*
3 cups chicken stock
1 cup cream
1 tsp salt
Pinch white pepper

Bring the first 4 ingredients to a boil and simmer for 25 minutes. Purée the mixture in a blender. Stir in white pepper, salt and cream. Serve soup hot or cold.

Raspberry Vinaigrette

3 cups oilve oil
1½ cups wine vinegar
2 cups raspberry syrup
3 tbls lemon juice
1 tsp salt
2 cups raspberries *(sieved to remove seeds)*

Mix and add seasonings such as celery salt and basil to taste. Salad is a mixture of green and red lettuce.

Drunken Chicken With Fresh Steamed Broccoli And Rosemary Roasted Potaotes

4 breasts of chicken *(boneless, skinless)*
3 cups bread crumbs
3 eggs
mild Vermont cheddar cheese
1 bottle golden sherry
3 cups flour
toothpicks

Pound chicken breasts, slightly. Slice Vermont cheddar into 1 inch thick pieces and place on ½ of chicken breast. Fold other side of chicken on top of the cheese and put a toothpick through each end. Dip both sides of chicken into flour, then dip into egg batter. Next, dip into bread crumbs until chicken is covered. Sauté both sides of chicken in a frying pan with a bit of oil, until both sides are brown. Remove chicken and toothpicks and place each chicken in a ceramic dish. Fill the dish with golden sherry, about ¼ cup, and bake at 400 degrees for approximately 30 minutes. Serve with fresh steamed broccoli and rosemary roasted potatoes.

Rosemary Roasted Potatoes:
4 whole potatoes
olive oil
Rosemary seasoning

Slice the potatoes into 1 inch thick pieces. Place the potato slice on a pan covered with olive oil. Turn the potatoes so they are covered with oil. Sprinkle rosemary over the potatoes and bake for 40 minutes at 400 degrees. Turn potatoes half way through cooking.

Apple Crisp

4-6 cups Granny Smith apples *(sliced)*
1 cup brown sugar
1 cup white sugar
1 cup oats
¾ tsp cinnamon
¾ tsp nutmeg
1 bottle pine nuts
1 cup melted butter

Heat oven to 375 degrees. Grease square pan and place apple slices in pan. Mix nuts, spices and white sugar in with apples. Mix brown sugar and oats together and sprinkle over apples. Pour butter over top and bake for 30 minutes. Serve warm in individual bowls and top with 2 scoops vanilla ice cream.

Wine Suggestion

Chardonnay, Chateau St. Michelle

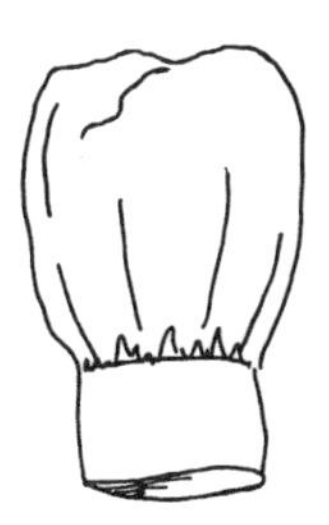

Meet The Highland House Chef Elise Durr

Chef Elise Durr enhances the classic character of *The Highland House* with traditional gourmet country cuisine. After working on Wall Street in New York City, Elise and her sister, a nurse, came to Vermont in the mid-seventies. Together, they own a bed and breakfast in Mt. Holly.

Dinners at *The Highland House* are served in the quaint six table post and beam dining room, accented by copper antiques. Memories are made here at intimate candlelight dinners.

Chef Durr and her sister have another important duty. They care for a sheep farm that is now a flock of 121 and Elise and Luise alternate two hour shifts during birthing times. Each lamb is given a name and the sisters can easily tell them apart by their personalities. The lambs are sold to people who want to keep their meadows clear and to provide wool and fresh meat in the fall.

Diners at *The Highland House* have come to enjoy the fresh, *homemade* breads, exquisite sauces and classical entrées such as the Drunken Chicken included in our Mountain Stirrings menus.

The Inn At Weston

A Heritage Of Excellence

Located on Route 100 in Weston, the Inn is comprised of several buildings, all typical of a small farming community of the nineteenth century. The buildings are listed on the National Register of Historic Places.The original inn building, which includes the dining room and pub, was built in 1848 as a working farmhouse with connecting stable and barn. It was first converted to a Guesthouse (now known as bed and breakfast inns) in the early 1950s and then became a full country inn in the early 1970s.

The Parkhurst House, built in 1895, is home to Innkeepers Jeanne and Bob Wilder. The Coleman House, across the street from the Inn, was built as a farmhouse in 1830 and has been recently renovated to offer additional guest rooms.

The Inn At Weston retains an informal atmosphere in keeping with its heritage while steadily developing a tradition of excellence in its dining and lodging facilities.

The Inn is recommended in nuerous guidebooks and has been featured in several national publications including *Gourmet* Magazine and on network television.

The Wilders purchased the Inn in 1985 after spending more than 20 years in corporate life. Prior to buying the inn, they lived in England for two years, travelling throughout Britain and Europe. They visited many inns and developed a taste for a less hectic life. After nine years of operating the Inn, they are pleased with that change in lifestyle.

The Inn At Weston
Route 100, Weston, Vermont 05161 (802) 824-6789

1. Tuna Time In Weston

On The Menu

Roesti Potato With Goat Cheese
Calamari Salad
Yellowfin Tuna With Pickled Ginger Wasabi Sauce
Lemon Tart With Blueberries

Roesti Potato With Goat Cheese

4 baking potatoes
6 oz goat cheese
salt and pepper *(to taste)*
chopped scallions

Boil potatoes 12 minutes in their skins. Cool 30 minutes and peel. Grate potatoes, and season with salt and pepper. Divide potatoes into 8 portions. Divide the cheese into 4 portions and place on 4 of the potato piles. Make a sandwich with the remaining potatoes. Pan fry in hot oil until golden brown on both sides. Finish in 450 degree oven 5 to 10 minutes. Garnish with chopped scallions.

Calamari Salad

1 lb small squid *(cleaned)*
2 cloves garlic
1 small red onion
1 jalapeno pepper *(finely minced)*
2 tbls red pepper *(chopped fine)*
2 tbls yellow pepper *(chopped fine)*
1 large tomato *(peeled, seeded and roughly chopped)*
2 tbls fresh lime juice
¼ cup plus 2 tbls extra virgin olive oil
¼ cup cilantro *(finely chopped)*
salt and pepper *(to taste)*

Cut squid bodies into ¼ inch rings and the tenticles into small pieces. In a sauté pan, heat the 2 tbls olive oil to medium hot. Sauté the squid for 1 minute until just opague. Meanwhile, mix the rest of the ingredients together in a bowl. Toss the squid with the vegetables and refrigerate for at least 1 hour. Serve on a lettuce leaf.

Yellowfin Tuna With Pickled Ginger Wasabi Sauce

4, 7 oz tuna steaks *(choose fish with bright color)*
½ cup sesame seeds
2 tbls black peppercorns *(coarsely crushed)*
salt *(to taste)*
3 egg yolks
2 tbls rice wine vinegar
2 cloves garlic
1 shallot

1 tbls fresh ginger *(chopped)*
2 tbls tamari sauce
8 oz peanut oil
juice of 1 lemon
1 cucumber *(peeled, sliced and diced into ¼ inch pieces)*
4 oz ginger *(pickled, julienned)*
2 tbls powdered wasabi *(moistened with cold water to form a stiff paste)*
¼ cup red pepper *(finely chopped)*
3 tbls cilantro *(finely chopped)*
1 tsp Chinese hot oil

In a food processor, place the garlic, fresh ginger, shallot, egg yolks, sesame oil, tamari, lemon juice, and rice vinegar. Process 10 seconds and then begin adding oil very slowly as in making a mayonnaise. Place in stainless steel bowl and add the rest of the ingredients. Season with salt and pepper if necessary. Refrigerate.

Mix the sesame seeds and pepper in a small bowl. Season the tuna with salt and roll into the seed mixture. In a sauté pan large enough to hold the 4 steaks, heat ¼ cup of peanut oil until very hot, but not smoking. Sear the tuna for 2-3 minutes on each side for rare. Garnish each steak with the sauce.

Lemon Tart With Blueberries

Sweet pastry:
8 oz. butter
2½ cup AP four *(unsifted)*
1/8 tsp salt
½ cup granulated sugar
1 large egg
1 tsp vanilla

Place the dry ingredients into the bowl of a food processor fitted with steel blade and process with 2-3 short on/off pulses to blend. Mix egg and vanilla in a small bowl just to combine. Cut the chilled butter into 12 pieces and scatter them over the dry ingredients. Process the butter and dry ingredients until the mixture resembles bread crumbs (about 15-20 seconds).

With the food processor running, pour the egg mixture down the feed tube and continue to process just until the ingredients come together. Remove the dough from the bowl and place it on a dry work surface. Then, with the heel of your hand, smear a small amount on your work surface by pushing it away from you. Repeat with small amounts of the remaining dough. When all dough has been worked, bring it together and divide into 2 potions and chill for at least 1 hour.

Filling:
2 large eggs
¾ cup granulated sugar
6 tbls lemon juice *(fresh)*
2 oz butter *(melted)*
2 tsp lemon zest
Fruit:
3 tbls apricot jam *(strained)*
2 cups blueberries *(fresh)*

Preheat oven to 375 degrees. Roll dough to a 12-inch circle, 1/8 inch thick. Place over a 9-inch quiche pan with removable bottom. Bake in pre-heated oven 10-12 minutes until it appears set. Check after 5-6 minutes to see if crust is blistering. If necessary, prick a few times to release steam. Place on cooling rack while filling is prepared.

Place eggs in small bowl and whisk just to combine. Pour in sugar and whisk. Add lemon juice, again whisking to combine. Add cooled butter and lemon zest and blend. Pour filling into the partially baked pie shell. Return to 375 degree oven and bake 16-18 minutes until crust is golden brown and filling is set. Remove and cool in rack for 10 minutes. Remove the metal rim from pan and cool.

Heat apricot jam just until hot. Pour into 2-quart mixing bowl. Pour blueberries over and mix gently. Spread over tart leaving a 3-inch portion in the center uncovered. Serve the same day for best flavor.

Wine Suggestion

William Hill Chardonnay Reserve, Napa Valley, California

2. A Rabbit At The Inn

On The Menu

Duck Liver And Fruit Pate
Grilled Portabella Mushroom Salad
Ragout Of Rabbit With Polenta
Cremé Brulee

Duck Liver And Fruit Pate

¾ cup dried apricots *(chopped)*
1/3 cup dried cranberries
juice of 4 oranges
2 tbls olive oil
2 tbls olive oil
2 tbls butter
2 large onions *(chopped)*
2 lbs duck livers *(cleaned and trimmed)*
6 oz bacon *(chopped)*
2 large apples *(peeled, cored and chopped)*
2 tbls fresh thyme
2 tbls parsley *(chopped)*
1 cup fresh breadcrumbs
½ cup heavy cream
juice of 1 lemon
2 eggs *(beaten)*
1 tbls green peppercorns *(crushed)*
¼ cup port wine

Place apricots and cranberries in a bowl. Pour in orange juice and let stands 2 hours to overnight. Heat burner and oil in large sauté pan over medium heat. Add onions and cook until transparent. Add liver and bacon and cook until lightly browned 5-10 minutes more. Mix in the apple, thyme and parsely and cook 2-3 minutes more.

Remove from heat and transfer to food processor. Process with bread crumbs, eggs, cream, and lemon juice and transfer to a large bowl. Stir in dried fruit with the remaining juice, peppercorns and port wine. Season to taste with salt and black pepper.

Line a terrine or loaf pan with parchment paper. Spoon the pate into the terrine and press in firmly. Cover with foil and place in a large roasting pan. Pour boiling water halfway up the side of the terrine. Bake in 350 degree over 1½ hours. Cool pate 1 hour on rack and then put weight on it to press it down firmly. Take the weight off after 1 hour and refrigerate overnight. Slice and serve with buttered toast points.

Grilled Portabella Mushroom Salad

1 lb Portabella mushroom caps *(stems removed)*
½ cup extra virgin olive oil
¼ cup sherry vinegar
1 tsp fresh rosemary *(chopped)*
salt and black pepper *(to taste)*
1 bunch arugula
1 bunch watercress
1 Belgian endive

Whisk together oil, vinegar, rosemary and salt and pepper to taste. Pour over the mushroom caps into an appropriate sized stainless steel bowl. Marinate mushrooms 1 hour, turning frequently. Grill mushrooms on a hot charcoal fire for 5 minutes, each side. Divide the cleaned greens onto four plates. Slice the mushrooms thin and place on the greens.

Ragout Of Rabbit With Polenta

1, 3 lb rabbit *(boned and cut into 1 inch pieces)*
1 onion *(finely chopped)*
4 oz dried apricots *(cut into 1/8 inch slices)*
8 oz slices chanterelle mushrooms
3 cloves garlic
3 tbls olive oil
4 oz Port wine
8 oz rich veal stock
1 tsp dry thyme
flour *(for dusting)*
salt and pepper *(to taste)*

Heat oil in a large sauté pan. Dust rabbit with flour and salt and pepper. Brown rabbit and place into an oven proof caserole. Add onions, garlic, mushrooms, and apricots to the sauté pan and cook on medium heat for 5 minutes. Deglaze the pan with the Port wine, and scrape the brown bits off the bottom. Add the veal stock and bring to a boil. Pour over rabbit and cover and bake in 350 degree oven for 45 minutes. Season if necessary. *(Serves 4 as an entree and 8 as an appetizer.)*

Polenta:
1 quart water
1 cup yellow corn meal
salt *(to taste)*
¼ cup mascarpone cheese
2 oz butter

Boil water with 1 tbls kosher salt. Add cornmeal very slowly, whisking vigorously. Cook on a low heat 45 minutes, stirring constantly. Add cheese and butter, and pour into a buttered 6-inch pan. Cover with wax paper and refrigerate 2 hours to overnight. Cut wedges out of polenta and heat 8 minutes in 400 degree oven. Spoon rabbit around polenta and garnish each with a sprig of fresh thyme.

Cremé Brulee

3 cups heavy cream
6 tbls sugar
6 egg yolks
2 tsp vanilla
¼ cup granulated sugar

Heat cream and sugar to scald. In a bowl, whisk egg yolks until light and fluffy. Slowly add cream mixture to the yolks, whisking briskly so as not to scramble the eggs. Add 2 tsp vanilla. Skim froth off top, and strain custard through a fine sieve. Pour into 4, 7½ oz ramikins and place them in a water bath. Cook in 300 degree oven 30-40 minutes until just set. Cool completely and sprinkle remaining sugar over the top of the four ramikins. Carmelize the sugar under a hot broiler or with propane torch. Cool 5 minutes and serve.

Wine Suggestion

Cameron Pinot Noir, Abbey Ridge Reserve, Willamette Valley, Oregon

Meet Inn At Weston Executive Chef Jay McCoy

Since the summer of 1985, Jay McCoy has served as Executive Chef of *The Inn At Weston.* He is largely responsible for the high quality and variety of the menu. Chef McCoy, together with Innkeepers Jeanne and Bob Wilder, plan the semi-annual menu updates. The chef also selects the daily specials based on seasonal factors and the availability of the freshest fish for his well-known variety of seafood delicacies.

Chef McCoy is a Pennsylvania native who has 22 years experience as a cook and chef. He is a graduate of the Culinary Institute of America and has led large country club kitchens in Philadelphia and Atlantic City before moving to Vermont with his family in the early 1980s.

He shares a love for the outdoors with his great love of cooking. His interest in wild mushrooms and other local products is constantly reflected in the menu at *The Inn At Weston.*

Mark Anthony's Ye Olde Tavern

A Place In History Where Patriots Dined

Nearly all of Vermont's founding fathers, those loyal to the King and the advocates of America's independence, have enjoyed the warm hospitality of *Ye Olde Tavern*. They arrived by stage from Boston and Albany, sipped wine in the tap room and enjoyed what became famous frontier food. They danced to the fiddler in the third floor ballroom and slept well in the lodging rooms. The Ames Livery in the Tavern Barn housed their horses and travelling gear.

Mark Anthony's *Ye Olde Tavern*, as we see it today, was built in 1790 by Aaron Sheldon, a fine East Rupert master carpenter, though the oldest parts date back to about 1760. The Colonial Georgian designed buidling is on the Register of Vermont Historic Places and is possibly one of the finest examples of surviving American architecture.

Its antiquity and size (4,500 square feet) make it unique. In an era when most people north of Massachusetts were living in log cabins, the "Old Tavern" appeared as a jewel in the wilderness. The nine pillars were later duplicated at the Equinox Hotel. Vermont was not yet a state in 1790, but rather a sovereign republic refused statehood by the "Yorkers."

Patriots such as Ethan Allen, Seth Warner, Ira Allen, Samuel Herrick, General St. Clair, Martin Powell, Major Gideon Ormsby and many others spent hours in the Tavern. In it's heyday, it was known as Thayer's Hotel.

Today, Mark Anthony Radicioni and his wife Diedre welcome visitors and locals alike to the newly re-named *Mark Anthony's Ye Olde Tavern.* Check our chef's profile at the end of this chapter to read more about Mark. Diedre is a cosmetologist who has run her own beauty salon and serves as full-time bookkeeper and hostess. She is a flower gardener with an interest in home restoration and decorating.

Mark Anthony's Ye Olde Tavern, Main Street, Manchester Ctr., Vermont 05255 (802) 362-0611; (800) 450-1790

---

1. Tongue At The Tavern

On The Menu

Salad Andolouse
Fresh Tongue With Blackberry Raisin Sauce,
Noodle Pancakes And Spinach And Mushroom Casserole
Orange Ice With Orange Sauce

Salad Andolouse

2 Spanish onions *(finely chopped)*
2 green peppers *(seeded, finely chopped)*
5 ripe tomatoes *(peeled, seeded, minced)*
salt and pepper *(to taste)*
oil
vinegar
chives *(finely chopped)*

In a salad bowl, arrange in layers Spanish onions, green peppers and tomatoes. Sprinkle each layer with salt and pepper. Pour over the vegetables a mixture of 3 parts oil to 1 part vinegar and chill the salad for at least 1 hour. Cover the top generously with chives.

Fresh Tongue With Blackberry Raisin Sauce, Noodle Pancakes And Mushroom Caps

4-5 lbs fresh beef tongue
3 celery stalks
1 onion
3 cloves
6 sprigs parsley
1 tbls salt
6 peppercorns

Wash beef tongue thoroughly and place in large kettle. Add celery stalks, onion stuck with cloves, parsley, salt and peppercorns. Add enough cold water to just cover the meat and bring the liquid slowly to a boil, skimming the surface frequently. Simmer tongue, covered, over low heat for about 3½ hours. Let tongue cool in stock. Drain it, peel off the skin. Trim away root and gristle. Cut tongue into slices and reheat. Then, slowly stir in blackberry raisin sauce.

Blackberry Raisin Sauce:
½ cup raisins
1 cup water
1 cup blackberry jelly
3 tbls lemon juice

In a saucepan, simmer raisins in 1 cup water for several minutes until they are plumped. Drain and stir in blackberry jelly and 3 tbls lemon juice. Heat sauce slowly. Stir constantly until jelly melts and sauce is well blackened. Do not let boil.

Noodle Pancakes:
8 oz package noodles *(very fine)*
2 eggs *(lightly beaten)*
¾ tsp salt
pinch pepper

Cook noodles in boiling salt water until tender. Drain thoroughly. In a bowl, mix noodles with eggs, salt and pepper. Put small mounds of noodle mixture on a generously buttered griddle and cook in the oven at moderate heat until the bottoms are golden brown. Turn with a spatula and brown other side. Serve immediately.

Spinach And Mushroom Casserole:
2 lbs spinach *(chopped coarsely)*
salt *(to taste)*
1 onion *(small, chopped)*
4 tbls butter
½ cup cheddar cheese *(grated)*
1 lb small mushrooms

Wash spinach. Drain and sprinkle lightly with salt. Cook spinach in the water that clings to the leaves for 4-5 minutes. Turn spinach into colander and press out as much water as possible, using the back of a water spoon. Chop spinach in bottom of a buttered shallow casserole (about 1½ inch deep) and sprinkle in with ½ cup cheddar. Cover spinach with mushrooms, trimmed and sautéed lightly in butter. Sprinkle with cheddar. Bake in moderate oven at 350 degrees for about 20 minutes until cheese is lightly browned.

Orange Ice With Orange Sauce

2 cans Mandarin oranges
sugar
Syrup:
4 cups water
2 cups sugar
2 cups orange juice
¼ cup lemon juice
2 oranges *(sections and finely grated rinds)*
1/3 cup orange-flavored liqueur

Drain oranges and measure the liquid. In a sauce pan, combine the liquid with an equal amount of sugar and cook it. Stir until sugar melts for about 3 minutes. Stir in liqueur and cook mixture 3 minutes longer. Pour mixture over orange sections and let chill over night.

Make a syrup by boiling 4 cups water with sugar for 5 minutes. Cool the syrup and add orange juice, lemon juice and the finely grated orange rind. Let mixture stand for about 10 minutes and strain into a large freezer tray. Freeze the ice until there is a firm border about 1 inch wide around the tray. Transfer the mix to a chilled bowl and beat it with an electric beater until smooth. Return mixture to refrigerator and freeze until firm.

Spoon orange ice into sherbet glasses and pour orange juice over the top. Serve immediately.

Wine Suggestion

Vermont Pear Wine *(dry),* North River Winery

2. Ye Olde Duck With Wine Sauce

On The Menu

Rock Lobster Tail
Duck With Wine Sauce And Caramelized Tomatoes
Molasses Candy Mousse

Rock Lobster Tails

6 small rock lobster tails
cucumbers *(thinly sliced)*

Put rock lobster tails unthawed in a kettle and cover with boiling salt water. Bring water to boil, cover and simmer for 5 minutes. Drain tails and when cool enough to handle, cut through thin undershell of each tail with scissors. Insert your finger through top shell and meat and pull out the meat in one piece. Reserve shells.

Chill the tail meat and cut into the shells, red side up. Serve on chilled platter with cucumbers. Pass around pink and green sauce.

Pink Sauce:
1 tbls tomato paste
1 pimiento
pinch tarragon
1 cup mayonnaise
dash tabasco
lemon juice *(to taste)*

Combine tomato paste and pimiento and stir. Drain. Add a pinch of tarragon and force mixture through a seive. Combine the purée with mayonnaise and tabasco. Add lemon juice.

Green Sauce:
parsley
watercress
chives
1 cup mayonnaise
1 tbls lemon juice

Blanch equal amounts of parsely, watercress and chives in hot water. Drain well and place in blender. Mix ¼ cup of the purée into 1 cup mayonnaise and 1 tbls lemon juice.

Duck With Wine Sauce And Caramelized Tomatoes

4 small duck halves
salt and pepper *(to taste)*
1/3 cup butter
¾ cup Port sherry or Madeira wine
12 slices orange rind
watercress *(garnish)*

Place duck halves on rack in roasting pan and sprinkle with salt and pepper. Roast in oven at 400 degrees for 20-25 minutes and drain off fat. Reduce oven temperature to 300 degrees and roast ducks, basting frequently for 1 to 1¼ hours or until tender.

Remove to a heated platter and keep warm. Drain off fat and melt butter in the baking pan. Stir in Port sherry or Madiera wine, orange rind slices. Cook over high heat until it is reduced to consistency of thin marmalade. Spoon sauce over duck and garnish with orange slice and watercress.

Caramelized Tomatoes:
6 medium tomatoes
3 slices white bread
1 cup tomato pulp
1 cup butter *(melted)*
1/3 cup brown sugar
¾ tsp salt
dash pepper

Cut a slice from the blossom end of tomatoes of uniform size and scoop out pulp with teaspoon. Reserve it. Put tomato shells in a shallow baking pan. Remove the crust from the bread and cut it into small cubes. In a bowl, combine the bread crumbs with tomato pulp, butter and brown sugar, salt and pepper. Fill tomato shells with mixture.Bake in 350 degree oven for about 30 minutes.

Molasses Candy Mousse

2 tbls flour
2 tbls sugar
pinch salt
1 cup milk
¼ lb chocolate covered molasses chips *(finely crushed with rolling pin)*
1 cup heavy cream *(firmly whipped)*

In a saucepan, mix 2 tbls each flour and sugar with salt. Stir in 1 cup milk gradually until it thickens. Let cool and chill. Stir in chocolate covered molasses chips. Fold in heavy cream and pour mixture into freezer tray. Cover tray with foil and freeze mousse until firm.

Wine Suggestion

Green Mountain Apple *(semi-dry)*, North River Winery

Meet Ye Old Tavern Chef Mark Anthony

Mark Radicioni has a long history of restaurant management experience in institutions, country clubs, large exclusive places and small family-owned restaurants. He has cooked as sous chef for Nouvelle Cuisine at the Franconia Inn in New Hampshire and at the Parker House Restaurant in Quechee, Vermont. He was the chef and owner of Brooksies Family Restaurant in Sharon, and the MarkAnthony Kettledrum in Fairlee, Vermont, businesses that are still in the family. He has been Executive Chef at the Sheraton North Country Inn at West Lebanon, New Hampshire and with the J.T.K. Management Company in Mystic, Connecticut. Chef Radicioni is well-known in the community as the operator of Grabber's Restaurant in Manchester for three years, before it was lost to fire in 1993.

His training includes attaining a Certificate of Mixology from Seagram 7 Corp., and an A.O.S. degree from the Culinary Institute of America. He has received awards from the American Skilled Olympics, Culinary Institute of America and the Executive Chef's Association.

Here in our community, Chef Radicioni is active in the Manchester Lions Club, Cub Scouts and youth sports programs.

Mistral's At Toll Gate

A Colorful History; A Reason To Tarry

Guests enjoy an elegant, intimate riverside setting and exquisite food at *Mistral's,* site of the last toll gate in Vermont. The private, five mile toll road was built in 1815 to link the towns of Peru and Manchester. Manchester residents Isaac Burton and Ephraim Munson and two men from Chester laid out the road and it was built by General Peter Dudley of Peru at a cost of $5,000. The slope was steep, the curves were many and the road was marked by 143 water bars. Those water bars were high mounds of packed earth placed across the road and ditched on the face to divert water and prevent wash-outs.

The Peru Turnpike, as it was known, became an important segment of the Boston-Saratoga stage route and travellers' fares were based upon the number of wheels on their carriages or the number of animals they were moving. A "wheeled pleasure carriage," for example, was 50 cents; a cart with two oxen, 20 cents and each horse and rider paid 6 cents.

Roads with water bars became obsolete with the advent of the automobile and the State of Vermont took responsibility for maintaining the Peru Turnpike by 1904, remaining in existence through 1917.

The building at the toll gate flourished as a private residence and later a lodge until Chef Mario Berry gave it formal recognition as Toll Gate Lodge, a rustic dining establishment with gourmet food and four-star service. Rock star Mick Jagger even celebrated his 40th birthday here.

After being closed for a while, the restaurant was refurbished by Dana and Cheryl Markey who renamed it Mistral's at Toll Gate for the cold wind that blows through the south of France. Dana is the chef while Cheryl oversees the dining room.

It is not uncommon for entertainment to include enjoying the sight of fish, heron and minks playing along the brook.

Enjoy *"A Winter Evening With Friends,"* a hearty meal to be enjoyed unhurried and amiably. Dana's second complete dinner is called *"A Summer Celebration"* inspired by the sunshine and blue skies of our Vermont summers.

Mistral's at Toll Gate, Toll Gate Road, Manchester Center, Vermont 05255 (802) 362-1779, (800) 279-1779

1. A Winter Evening With Friends

On The Menu

Pappardelle With Portabello Mushrooms
Warm Grilled Shrimp Salad With Mustard Garlic Vinaigrette
Medallions Of Venison With Port And Sun Dried Cherry Sauce
Poached Pears Baumes-de-Venise

Pappardelle With Portabello Mushrooms

1 lb fresh Pappardelle *(pasta sheets cut into 1"x2" rectangles)*
2 lbs fresh portabello mushrooms *(stemmed and thinly sliced)*
½ lb spinach, stem and chiffonade *(cut leaves into coarse shreds)*
1 tbsp shallots *(minced)*
1 tsp parsley *(minced)*
3 oz brandy
¼ cup chicken stock
salt and pepper
1 tsp garlic *(minced)*
6 tsp unsalted butter
3 oz dry sherry
4 oz Asiago cheese *(shaved)*
Pasta ingredients:
1 cup Semolina flour
1 cup all-purpose flour
3 eggs
2 tbsp olive oil
pinch of salt

Bring 6 qts. water to a rolling boil with 1 tbsp. of salt. While water comes to a boil, prepare sauce. In a large sauté pan, sauté 3 tbsp. butter with mushrooms, shallots, garlic and spinach over high heat. Flambé with brandy and sherry *(and, use care, mixture will flame)*. Add chicken stock. Cook until mixture is reduced by half. Reduce heat. Whisk in remaining butter. Salt and pepper to taste. Cook pappardelle in boiling water for 2-3 minutes for al dente pasta *(pasta is slightly firm)*. Drain pasta well. Toss with sauce. Divide into four shallow pasta bowls and sprinkle with Asiago cheese. Garnish with chopped parsley. Serve immediately.

To make pasta: In a food processor with a steel blade, blend for 30 seconds. Add a few drops of water, a little at a time, until dough forms a ball. Let rest. Roll out dough as thinly as possible on a floured surface. Cut into 1"x2" rectangles. Or, buy fresh pasta sheets.

Warm Grilled Shrimp Salad with Mustard Garlic Vinaigrette

½ lb mesclun *(or any fresh, baby lettuces if not available)*
1 lemon cut into 4 wedges
8-12 jumbo shrimp *(2-3 per person)*, peeled and deveined
Shrimp Marinade:
2 tbsp Dijon mustard

½ tsp fresh ginger
2 oz dry sherry
1 tbsp olive oil
Vinaigrette:
2 tbsp white wine vinegar
1 tbsp dry sherry
1 tbsp Dijon mustard
1 garlic clove *(crushed)*
½ cup light olive oil
pinch of black pepper

Combine ingredients for shrimp marinade in mixing bowl. Add shrimp and marinate for 30 minutes. While shrimp are marinating, clean and spin mesclun and prepare dressing. Combine all ingredients (except olive oil) in mixing bowl. Whisk in a slow stream of olive oil carefully. Toss mesclun with half of the vinaigrette mixture.

Grill shrimp over high heat 3-4 minutes on each side. Keep warm. Arrange mesclun on four plates. Place 2-3 shrimp on each plate and drizzle with remaining vinaigrette dressing. Garnish with lemon wedges. Serve immediately.

Medallions of Venison With Port And Sun Dried Cherry Sauce

8, 2½ to 3½ oz. medallions of venison *(cut from the saddle)* about ¾" thick. Allow two medallions per person.
Sauce:
½ cup sun dried cherries
¾ cup Port
½ tsp garlic *(minced)*
olive oil
2 tsp unsalted butter *(optional)*
1 tsp shallots *(minced)*
½ cup demi-glace
salt and pepper

Marinate cherries in Port for 30 minutes. Save 1 oz Port for deglazing. In a large sauté pan, sear the medallions in 2 oz. olive oil over high heat for 3-4 minutes on each side for a medium rare medallion. Keep warm.

Pour off liquid in pan and add remaining port to deglaze. Add butter, garlic, shallots and briefly sauté. Add cherries and port marinade and cook until reduced by one-third. Add demi-glace and reduce until slightly thickened. Salt and pepper to taste. Swirl in butter, if desired.

Top each medallion with port and sun dried cherry sauce. Serve with roasted new potatoes, caramelized onions, steamed baby carrots and haricots verts.

Poached Pears Baumes-de-Venise

4 ripe, peeled Bartlett pairs
1 cinnamon stick
½ cup sugar
375 ml Muscat, Baumes-de-Venise, *(Jaboulet Aîné)*

1 orange *(juice and peel)*
vanilla ice cream

In saucepan, combine wine, cinnamon stick, sugar and orange. Bring to boil. Add pears. Reduce heat and cover, simmer for 30 minutes or until tender. Remove pears with slotted spoon. Cool. Remove core with apple corer. Refrigerate.

Godiva Chocolate Sauce:
6 oz Callebaut bittersweet chocolate *(coarsely chopped)*
½ cup heavy cream
2 oz Godiva Chocolate Liqueur

Scald heavy cream. In a small sauce pan, pour cream over chocolate. Stir until smooth. Add Godiva liqueur and keep warm. Stuff pear with vanilla ice cream. Place pear on dessert plate and drench with chocolate sauce. Garnish with fresh raspberries.

Wine Suggestion

1988 Chateau Pichon Longueville Baron or 1991 Williams-Selyem Pinot Noir.

2. A Summer Celebration

On The Menu

Maine Crab Cakes Grenobloise
Tomato Mozzarella Salad With Basil Balsamic Vinaigrette
Fresh Rainbow Trout Stuffed With Salmon Mousse, Chardonnay Dill Sauce
Coupe Mistral

Maine Crab Cakes Grenobloise

1 small onion
4 celery stalks
1-2 tbsp unsalted butter
1 lb fresh Maine crabmeat
1 cup fresh bread crumbs
3 tbsp parsley *(minced)*
2 eggs
1 lemon
1 cup bread crumbs *(toasted)*
3-4 tbsp clarified butter

Finely mince onion and celery and sauté in 1 tbsp. butter. Let cool in a large stainless steel bowl. Flake crabmeat while removing all shells and cartilage Add sautéed celery and onion along with fresh bread crumbs, parsley, eggs *(slightly beaten)*, juice of one lemon. Mix thoroughly. Season to taste with salt and pepper. Form mixture into 8 cakes about 2" round, ¾" thick. Coat cakes with finely ground toasted bread crumbs. Sauté cakes in 2-3 tbsp. clarified butter over medium high heat. Lightly brown on each side and place on oven-proof platter. Bake at 450 degrees for 10-12 minutes or until heated throughout. Place two cakes on each plate and top with Sauce Grenobloise and lemon wedges. Serve immediately.

Sauce Grenobloise:
1 tbsp shallots *(minced)*
3-4 tbsp unsalted butter
3-4 tbsp non-pariel capers
1 oz brandy
2 oz white wine
6-8 oz veal or chicken stock
parsley *(minced)*
lemon

Sauté shallots in 1 tbsp. butter until translucent over high heat. Add capers, brandy *(be careful, it will flare)* and wine. Reduce by half and add stock. Reduce again by half and add lemon juice and parsley. With heat off, swirl remaining butter into sauce. Adjust seasonings. Keep warm.

Tomato Mozzarella Salad With Basil Balsamic Vinaigrette

2 large vine-ripened tomatoes
2 tbsp fresh basil *(minced)*
black pepper (fresh ground)
½ lb fresh mozzarella cheese
2 tbsp balsamic vinegar
1 clove garlic *(minced)*
½ cup olive oil
½ cup Olives de Provence

To make dressing: In mixing bowl, combine vinegar, garlic, basil . Whisk in olive oil. Season to taste. Slice tomatoes and mozzarella cheese in equal thickness about ¼ to ½" thick. Arrange on salad plate, alternating tomato and cheese in a circular fan. Spoon dressing over tomatoes and cheese. Garnish with olives and fresh basil sprig.

Fresh Rainbow Trout Stuffed With Salmon Mousse, Chardonnay Dill Sauce

4 fresh boneless rainbow trout *(head and fins removed)*
2 oz clarified butter
flour
salt and pepper

For Salmon Mousse:
4 oz fresh salmon
1 egg
½ tsp fresh dill
1 tsp shallots *(minced)*
1 egg yolk
2 oz heavy cream

For Chardonnay Dill Sauce:
2 tbsp unsalted butter
1 oz brandy
2 oz lobster stock
1 tbsp dill *(chopped)*
1 tbsp shallots
3 oz Chardonnay
3 oz heavy cream

To make Salmon Mousse: In food processor with steel blade, process salmon and shallots. Add egg and egg yolk, one at a time. Scrape bowl to thoroughly blend. Slowly add cream with machine on. Add dill; salt and pepper to taste. Refrigerate until needed.

Season the trout *(inside)* with salt and pepper. Stuff with Salmon Mousse mixture. Carefully dredge trout in flour and sauté in clarified butter over high heat until lightly browned on each side. Place trout in 425 degree oven for 10-12 minutes. It should be firm to the touch. Remove from oven. Let rest. While trout is in the oven, sauté shallots in butter over high heat. Flambé with brandy. Add chardonnay. Reduce by half. Add lobster stock and reduce. Add cream and reduce until slightly thickened. Add fresh dill and season to taste.

Carefully remove skin from trout. Place on platter and spoon sauce over trout. Serve with steamed broccoli and baby carrots.

Coupe Mistral

1 qt coffee ice cream
1 cup hazelnuts *(Filberts, chopped)*
1 cup hot fudge sauce *(your favorite)*
4 oz Frangelico liqueur
4-6 oz whipped heavy cream or whipped topping for garnish
1 oz chocolate shavings *(optional)*

Toast chopped hazlenuts on cookie sheet in 350-degree oven for 6-8 minutes with ice cream scoop. With ice cream scoop, form coffee ice cream into 4 balls, each about the size of a tennis ball with ice cream scoop. Roll in cooled hazlenuts and return to freezer.

To Serve: Place 2 oz hot fudge sauce into large red wine goblet or dessert bowl. Place each rolled ice cream ball on top of fudge sauce and add 1 oz of Frangelico liqueur. Garnish with whipped cream and chocolate shavings. Serve with cappuccino or expresso.

Wine Suggestion

1991 Mondavi Fumé Blanc Reserve or 1992 Frog's Leap Chardonnay

Meet Mistral's At Toll Gate Chef Dana Markey

A Manchester, Vermont native, Dana Markey has been cooking in this region for many years before discovering a place to call his own. With his wife, Cheryl, as his partner, *Mistral's at Toll Gate* has become a labor of love.

From the early renovations to the roof-top shoveling, it is difficult to separate the restaurant from his way of life. While Dana enjoys skiing and playing golf, he spends most of his time in the *Mistral's* kitchen cooking for his biggest fans, the women in his life, including his wife and their two daughters. The Markey family lives above the kitchen and the children have learned their lessons well in terms of the rewards such proximity can bring as special desserts and treats.

Coming from a French and Italian background and from a family that loved to cook, eat and entertain, his cuisine leans toward the classical, but many a salsa has escaped this French kitchen. If Dana has a special trait, it is accommodation, wishing only to create something of a delicious pleasure for his customers. He uses only the finest, fresh products and the time and care he gives to each plate comes only from a man who cooks from his heart.

It is only fitting that *Mistral's* should be located in such a romantic and naturally beautiful riverside setting. As Bromley Brook cascades through the mossy flume and trout make their way upstream, Chef Markey allows his diners to savor a little taste of pure inspiration.

The Reluctant Panther

A Truly Unique Atmosphere In Vermont

Set among the towering trees, white clapboard mansions and the shadow of Mount Equinox, *The Reluctant Panther* offers a unique, special atmosphere like none other in Vermont. The unusual mauve color highlighted by bright yellow shutters, has made *The Reluctant Panther* a landmark in Manchester Village. Built in the 1850s, the three story main house was once the home of a wealthy merchant. It became an inn nearly 40 years ago and has recently been totally refurbished with new suites added.

Each guest room is individually decorated and all have private bath, air conditioning, telephone and cable TV, some with fireplaces. The beautiful Mary Porter House, adjacent to the inn, includes four suites with whirlpool, fireplaces, air conditioning and classic four-poster beds. And, each guest is welcomed to their room with a bottle of Robert Mondavi wine.

Wildflowers is an intimate gourmet restaurant at The Reluctant Panther, where fine crystal and china reflect a warm glow from the fireplace. Sunlight gives the *Greenhouse* a special warmth and this private dining area is ideal for morning coffee or a quiet evening dinner.

Innkeeper Robert Bachofen was trained in hotel management in Switzerland and before coming to Vermont in 1989, he was in the top managemenr echelon of New York's famed Plaza Hotel. His wife Maye is also trained in hotel management and the pair are ready to greet guests who might be reluctant only once.

Chef Karen Strand constantly surprises visitors with wonderful appetizers, unusual entrees and spectacular desserts.

The Reluctant Panther, West Road,
Manchester Village, Vermont 05254 (802) 362-2568; (800) 822-2331

1. Roasted Rack Of Venison For The Panther

On The Menu

Marinated And Grilled Portabello Mushrooms Served
With Port Wine And Creme Fraiche.
Roasted Rack Of Venison With Cranberry Gravy And Purée Of Carrots
Fig Tart With Cointreau Creme Anglaise

Marinated And Grilled Portabello Mushrooms Served With Port Wine And Creme Fraiche

Marinate:
4 large Portabello mushrooms
2 cups blended oil
¼ cup Balsamic vinegar
2 tbls coarse black pepper

Bring the oil to a boil *(375 degrees)* and remove from heat. Add vinegar, pepper, salt and let cool. Remove and discard the stem and ribs of mushrooms. Add mushrooms to mixture and marinate for three hours.

Port Wine Creme Fraiche:
1 cup Creme Fraiche or sour cream
1 cup demi-glace or 1, 16 oz can of beef bouillon
3 shallots
2 cups Port wine

Combine the demi-glace or beef bouillon, shallots and Port wine. Reduce to 1/3 of original amount over high heat. Cool and combine with creme fraiche or sour cream. When ready to serve, sear mushrooms lightly in sauté pan or on grill approximately 1 minute on each side. Serve with generous dollop of creme fraiche.

Roasted Rack Of Venison With Cranberry Gravy And Purée Of Carrots

2 full racks of venison *(4 ribs per person)*
¼ cup blended oil
4 bulbs shallots *(minced)*
4 tsp parsely *(minced)*
1 cup plain bread crumbs
salt and pepper *(to taste)*

Pre-heat oven to 375 degrees. Heat oil in pan until almost smoking. Season venison with salt and pepper. Sear the racks on both sides in hot oil. Combine shallots, parsley and bread crumbs. Press mixture on both sides of racks and roast in oven for 35 minutes for rare to medium-rare. Serve immediately with gravy.

Cranberry Gravy:
1 can whole cranberries
3 bulbs roasted shallots
½ cup peeled pearl onions
1 cup demi glace (or 1 oz can beef bouillon thickened with 1 tbls roux and reduced by half.

Combine all ingredients in sauté pan and cook for 10 minutes.

Purée of Carrots:
1½ lbs peeled, sliced carrots
1 cup water
¼ cup brown sugar
½ lb butter *(browned)*

Pre-heat oven to 350 degrees. Combine carrots, water and brown sugar in baking pan. Cover and bake 40-50 minutes or until tender. Lightly brown butter in sauté pan on stove. Add butter to carrots and purée in food processor.

Fig Tart With Cointreau Creme Anglaise

1 cup fig jam
12 large ripe fresh figs *(quartered)*

Walnut Crust Tart Shell (9 inch):
6 oz finely chopped walnuts
½ cup *(1 stick)* butter *(unsalted at room temperature)*
¼ cup sugar *(granulated)*
1½ cup AP flour
1 egg yolk *(lightly beaten)*
½ tsp vanilla extract

Pre-heat oven to 350 degrees. Butter and flour tart pan. Place all tart shell ingredients in mixing bowl and mix until well-blended. Press mixture into tart pans and chill for 30 minutes. Bake crust for 20-25 minutes or until golden brown. Cool before filling.

Pastry cream:
1 cup milk
¼ cup granulated sugar
3 tbls A.P. flour
¼ tsp salt
4 egg yolks *(lightly beaten)*
2 tsp vanilla extract
2 tbls butter *(unsalted)*

Heat milk. Do not boil. Combine sugar, flour and salt and slowly add hot milk. Bring to boil over low heat, stirring constantly. Cook until smooth and very thick. Take off heat and beat in yolks, one at a time. Return to heat and boil for one minute, stirring constantly. Take off heat and stir in butter and vanilla until well mixed. Cover surface with plastic wrap and cool.

To assemble: Spread jam over bottom of tart shell. Spread an even layer of pastry cream over jam. Arrange quartered figs over pastry cream. Serve chilled.

Cointreau Creme Anglaise:
2½ cups milk
¾ cup sugar
6 egg yolks
2 tsp cornstarch
1 vanilla bean (split and scraped)
2 tbls cointreau

Boil milk and vanila bean for one minute. Remove bean. Beat yolks and sugar until thick and fluffy. Add cornstarch. Temper in hot milk a little at a time. Place in metal bowl over boiling water and stir until a light creamy consistency. Do not let boil. Remove from heat and stir in cointreau. Strain through fine sieve and cool. Refrigerate until ready to use.

Wine Suggestion

1988 Medoc, Chateaux Calon-Segur

2. A Spicy Thai Shrimp Dinner

On The Menu

Baked Tart Of Chevre With Leeks, Walnuts And Elephant Garlic
Grilled Vegetables On Watercress With Japanese Vinaigrette
Spicy Thai Shrimp With Red Curry, Cocoanut Milk And Potatoes
Served Over Fresh Pasta
Lime Tart With Poppy seed Crust Served With Raspberry Sauce, Whipped Cream

Baked Tart Of Chevre With Leeks, Walnuts And Elephant Garlic

For one 8-inch tart:
1, 8-inch tart shell *(pre-baked)*
1 head elephant garlic *(or regular garlic)*
3 egg yolks
1 lb goat cheese
¼ lb leeks *(cleaned well and sliced)*
½ cup heavy cream
½ cup walnuits
2-3 tomatoes *(for garnish)*

Pre-heat oven to 350 degrees. Rub garlic with some oil, wrap in foil and roast for 1 hour. Cool garlic and press cloves out of their skins. Take 2 cloves elephant garlic *(or 1 head regular garlic)* and place in food processor. Sauté leeks in a bit of oil until tender and cool. Add egg yolks, goat cheese, leeks, walnuts and cream to garlic and purée. Turn oven up to 375 degrees. Pour mixture into pre-baked tart shell and bake for 35-40 minutes. Slice tomatoes and place around edge of tart, overlapping slightly. Bake for ten minutes more. Test for doneness as you would a cake. Allow to cool and set before serving.

Grilled Vegetables On Watercress With Japanese Vinaigrette

1 lb watercress *(cleaned)*
1 zucchini *(cut on bias ¼ thick)*
1 yellow squash *(cut on bias ¼ thick)*
4 plum tomatoes *(cut on bias ¼ thick)*
2 Japanese eggplants *(or, 1 small regular eggplant cut on bias ¼ thick)*
1 red onion *(sliced into rings, ¼ inch thick)*
Marinade:
½ cup soy sauce
1 tbls fresh ginger *(minced)*
2 tbls Hoisin sauce
2 tbls sesame seeds *(lightly toasted)*
Vinaigrette:
1 cup blended oil
½ cup rice wine vineger
½ tbls prepared wasabi
3 tbls lemon juice
2 tbls lime juice
1 tsp crushed red pepper
4 oz soy or tamari sauce
1 tsp ginger *(fresh, minced)*
1 tsp garlic *(fresh, minced)*
½ cup sesame seeds *(lightly toasted)*

Combine marinade ingredients. Marinate the sliced vegetables for ½ hour. Grill until cooked, but not soggy and let cool. Combine all dressing ingredients in a food processor except the oil and sesame seeds. Turn on machine and slowly pour in oil until well-blended. Toss salad greens with grilled vegetables or arrange vegetables over the greens in a decorative pattern. Drizzle with dressing and sprinkle with sesame seeds.

Spicy Thai Shrimp With Red Curry, Coconut Milk And Tomatoes Served Over Fresh Pasta

1¼ lb jumbo shrimp *(peeled and diced)*
2 scallions *(chopped)*
1 tbls shallots *(minced)*
1 tbls ginger *(fresh, minced)*
1 tbls garlic *(fresh, minced)*
2 tbls Thai curry paste
1 cup dry white wine
¼ cup heavy cream
2, 16 oz cans coconut milk
2 tbls blended oil
salt, and pepper *(to taste)*
fresh pasta *(your choice)*

Sauté shrimp in oil for 2-3 minutes with shallots, scallions, garlic and ginger. Add coconut milk and slowly simmer for 5 more minutes. In another pan, bring wine to a boil and add curry paste and tomatoes. Simmer 2 minutes and add to shrimp.

Simmer 5 minutes. Add cream and take off heat. Do not boil! Pour over pasta cooked al denté *(firm, not soft)* and serve.

Lime Tart With Poppy Seed Crust
Served With Raspberry Sauce And Whipped Cream

Crust:
1½ cup AP flour
¼ cup sugar
pinch salt
10 tsp cold unsalted butter *(cut into small pieces)*
1 egg yolk *(mixed with 1 tbls cold water)*
¼ cup poppy seeds

Combine dry ingredients and poppy seeds in food processor. Pulse to mix. Add butter and pulse until butter is in pea-sized particles. With machine running, add egg yolk mixture and mix until dough just comes together. Form into ball with hands; wrap in saran and refrigerate at least an hour. Roll out chilled dough to thickness of ¼ inch and place in buttered and floured tart shell. Prick bottom of tart with fork and refrigerate ½ hour or until firm.

Place foil over tart shell with beans or pie weights and bake in 400 degree oven for 10 minutes. Remove foil and cook for additional 10-12 minutes until lightly browned. Cool.

Filling:
6 egg yolks
1¼ cup sugar
2 tsp cornstarch
½ cup lime juice
zest of limes used for juice

Whip yolks and sugar in mixer or by hand for 2 minutes. Combine cornstarch, lime juice and zest. Stir well and imediately add to egg yolk mixture and whip for 2 minutes. Pour into tart shell and bake for 30 minutes at 350 degrees. Tent with foil if it becomes too brown. Let cool at room temperature. Refrigerate for at least 3 hours before serving.

Wine Suggestion

Gewurztraminer, Chateaux St. Michelle

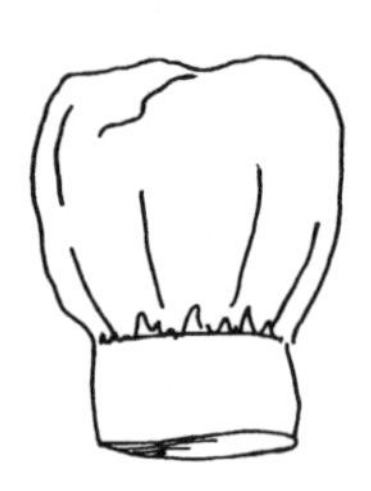

Meet Reluctant Panther Chef Karen Strand

Chef Karen Strand of *The Reluctant Panther* is a graduate of the Culinary Institute of America. Her inn career began with the Barrows House in Dorset where she was Assistant Innkeeper before moving to Aspen, Colorado to work as pastry chef at the resort's famed Little Nell. Returning to Vermont in 1993, she became Sous Chef at *The Reluctant Panther* and was named to top role in summer, 1994.

Before getting involved in the kitchen world, Karen spent a decade working with physically and mentally disabled persons in a therapeutic capacity. She enjoys floral design, graphic arts, computer work, herb and vegetable gardening and speaks two foreign languages.

Three Clock Inn

Fine Dining In A 200-Year-Old Farmhouse

Londonderry's *Three Clock Inn* is a 200-year-old farm house that Clayton and Helen Curtis first turned into an inn in 1959. Patricia McNeur owned the inn in the early 1960s and opened the restaurant. She also sold food on a "take-out" basis from its kitchen.

Patricia named the inn for the three antique, clockmaker signs she had hanging on the living room wall. Hank and Frances Tschernitz purchased the inn from Patricia and continued to operate it as a very successful fine dining establishment and sold it to Lisa Patton Brown in 1992.

Lisa was born and raised in Memphis, Tennessee and is a graduate of the University of Alabama. She served as Promotion Manager for WMC-FM radio and WMC-TV in Memphis and managed the Orpheum Theatre before buying the inn. She has two children, Michael, 6, and William, 4, who assist as junior innkeepers.

Three Clock Inn, Middletown Road

So. Londonderry, Vermont 05148, (802) 824-6327

1. Bifsteak Au Londonderry

On The Menu

Escargot
Tossed Fresh Garden Green Salad
Bifsteak Au Poivre With Sauce Espagnole
Strawberries Romanoff

Escargot

24 snails and shells *(Indonesian or French)*
1/8 cup shallots *(chopped)*
1/8 cup garlic *(chopped)*
1/8 cup parsley
lb butter *(slightly salted and softened)*
2 dashes tabasco sauce
1 tsp lemon juice
nutmeg *(to taste)*
salt *(to taste)*

Mix garlic, shallots, butter, lemon juice and seasonings together. Stuff shells first with butter, then snail, then more butter mixture. Cook in oven at 400 degrees for 7-8 minutes. Sprinkle with parsley.

Tossed Garden Green Salad

Use fresh garden greens such as Romaine for firmness, arrugala with a sliver of sliced Belgian endive. Brush with olive oil and taragon vinegar and use fresh cracked pepper to taste.

Bifsteak Au Poivre With Sauce Espagnole

4 tbls butter
2 shallots *(finely chopped)*
1 cup Sauce Espagnole
1/3 cup dry red wine
¼ cup cracked pepper
4 filet mignon (1½-2 inches thick)
salt and pepper *(to taste)*
¼ cup beef broth
2 tbls Cognac *(optional)*
4 rounds of fried toast

Melt 1 tbls butter in saucepan and brown shallots. Add Sauce Espagnole and wine. Simmer for 15 minutes, skimming as needed. Press pepper into both sides of meat. Heat remaining 3 tbls butter to sizzling in a large frying pan and sear filets for 4 minutes on each side for rare. Season with salt. Reserve and keep hot.

Deglaze frying pan with beef broth and pour into sauce. Add cognac to sauce *(optional)* and simmer for five minutes. Place beef on fried toast on a heated serving platter. Pour 1 tbls sauce over each filet. Pass sauce in a sauce boat.

Sauce Espagnole:
2 tbls butter
1 onion *(finely chopped)*
1 small carrot *(diced)*
Bouquet garni *(1 bay leaf, ½ tsp dried thyme, 4 peppercorns, parsley sprigs, tied in cheesecloth)*
½ cup dry white wine
3 cups brown sauce
2 cups beef broth
2 tbls tomato paste
salt and pepper *(to taste)*

Melt butter in saucepan and cook onion, carrot until soft and browned. Add boquet garni, wine, brown sauce and 1 cup broth. Simmer for 1 hour, skimming with care. Strain into a clean saucepan, add tomato paste and remaining broth, and stir well. Simmer for ¾ hour, skimming as before. Season to taste and strain again.Use as directed or cool and store in refrigerator. Makes about 4 cups.

Brown Sauce:
2 tbls butter
2 tbls flour
2 cups beef broth or stock
1 tbls tomato purée *(optional)*
salt and pepper *(to taste)*

Heat butter until hot and boiling. Stir in flour until smooth. Fry slowly until mixture turns medium brown. Slowly stir in broth and bring to boil. Reduce heat and simmer 20-25 minutes or until smooth and thickened. Stir in tomato purée, salt and pepper and simmer 5-10 minutes longer. Makes 2 cups.

Strawberries Romanoff

1, 6 oz package strawberries *(frozen)*
1 pint heavy cream *(firmly whipped)*
1 oz Grand Marnier liqueur
1 oz Port wine
½ pint strawberries *(fresh, cut into pieces)*
2 scoops vanilla ice cream
rinds of 1 lemon *(whole)*
rinds of 1 orange *(whole)*

Stir all ingredients together and garnish with fresh strawberries. Store in refrigerator. Soak rinds of whole lemon and orange in wine and Grand Marnier mixture. Let soak 1 hour and discard rinds.

Wine Suggestion

1990 Chateau Larose-Trintaudon or 1989 Jordan Cabernet Sauvignon

2. Bass In The Mountains

On The Menu

Stracciatello á la Romana
Caesar Salad
Sarapicca Of Striped Bass
Banana Flambé

Stracciatello á la Romana

6 cups chicken consomme
1 egg *(whipped)*
¼ cup semolina flour
¼ cup Parmesan *(fresh, grated)*
pinch nutmeg
parsley *(fresh, for sprinkling)*

Bring chicken consomme to boil. Drop in egg with mixture of Parmesan cheese, nutmeg and semolina flour. Boil 3 minutes, stirring constantly. Sprinkle with parsley.

Caesar Salad

½ cup Parmesan cheese
1 egg
1 head Romaine lettuce
olive oil *(soaked with 1 tbls chopped garlic, or more if you wish)*
crutons
3 anchovie filets
2 dashes Lea and Perrins Worcestershire sauce
2 dashes tabasco sauce
3 tbls red wine vinegar *(to taste)*
1 tsp fresh horseradish *(to taste)*
pepper *(ground, coarse)*

Mold anchovies into paste. Add Worcestershire sauce, horseradish, red wine vinegar and tabasco to pastes and mix together in a small bowl. Soak crutons in olive oil. Boil egg for 2 minutes. In wooden bowl, combine lettuce, anchovie mixture and crutons. Drop egg into bowl. Sprinkle with parmesan cheese and pepper. Mix well and serve.

Sarapicca Of Striped Bass

24 oz striped bass
2 oz Roquefort cheese
8 oz Philadelphia cream cheese *(blended with Roquefort to make paste)*
4 large raw shrimp
8 medium pitted black olives *(split)*
strips of red pepper
dry white wine

aluminum foil *(4 pieces)*
8 thin slices of lemon

Place 1 filet of bass on 1 piece of aluminum foil, moistened with 1 tbls white wine underneath the fish. Place ¼ cheese paste on top of filet. Put 1 shrimp, slit in half, on top of cheese. Place lemon slices, olives and red pepper slices on top. Fold aluminum foil, air tight, around fish and bake at 400 degrees for 20 minutes or until cooked.

Bananas Flambé

4 bananas *(sliced lengthwise)*
1 tsp butter *(to cover bottom of pan)*
1 tsp brown sugar
vanilla ice cream
3 oz Applejack
1 pint heavy cream *(whipped)*

Heat skillet with butter and lightly sauté banana. Add sugar and flambé with applejack. After flame dies, serve bananas over vanilla ice cream with whipped cream.

Wine Suggestion

Kendall Jackson Chardonnay

Meet Three Clock Inn Chef Heinrich Tschernitz

Born and raised in Linz, Austia, Chef Tschernitz moved to the United States in 1959, after working in Caracas, Venezuela, Stockholm, Sweden and in Switzerland. Chef Tschernitz came to Vermont in 1960 and became head waiter of the Toll Gate Lodge (now Mistral's At Toll Gate). In fact, he met his wife, Frances at the Toll Gate Lodge and they were married in 1966. The pair bought *Three Clock Inn* from Patricia McNeur in 1968.

A loyal following comes to *Three Clock Inn* to contiue sample the fine cuisine prepared by this well-known gourmet chef.

The Village Fare

Informal Dining In Historic Manchester

The building that currently plays host to the *Village Fare* restaurant has a history dating back to 1865 when it was built by C.W. Orvis. At that point in time, it sat between the Music Hall and what is now the Orvis Gift Shop. Records indicate the building was sold to L.D. Coy who used all three floors of the building.

The basement level was used to produce boots, shoes and other leather goods. The first floor, now the cafe, was the boot and shoe shop. The second floor served as a dentist's office and a YMCA room.

Coy sold to H.S. Dow, who turned the store into a grocery and general store. It's not clear when the building was moved, but whenever that physical move was made, a small addition to the back was added. Leon Wiley took over in 1919 and it remained Wiley's Store until 1975. Today, the building is owned by Equinox Hotel and Resort. A Vermont Products store occupied the space and in 1988, the building became a restaurant.

The present proprietors, Ken Farrell and Paula Sweeney bought the property in October, 1993, added more seats, installed a very special bakery and began to welcome guests to *Village Fare.*

Village Fare, Union Street,
Manchester Village, Vermont 05254 (802) 362-2599

1. Black Beans And Chili In The Village

Poblano Chilies Stuffed With Crab And Avacado
Black Bean Chili With Jalapeno Corn Corn Bread
Polenta Almond Pound Cake with Fresh Berries

Poblano Chilies Stuffed With Crab And Avacado

12 peppers
Filling:
2, 6½ oz. cans crab met *(drain)*
2 tsp onions *(minced)*
2 ripe avocados *(chopped)*
1 cup Belgium endive *(chopped)*
1 tsp cilantro *(fresh)*
1 red pepper *(diced)*
Vinaigrette:
1 cup rice wine vinegar
1½ cup olive oil
½ ground pepper *(fresh)*
2 tsp oregano
2 lbs red onions *(thinly sliced)*

Roast and peel peppers. Cut lengthwise on one side, remove seeds and ribs. Set aside. Drain crab meat. Mix in onions, avocados, endive, colantro and red pepper. Fill each pepper until just overflowing. Top with vinaigrette. Refrigerate 24 hours before serving.

Black Bean Chili with Jalapeno Corn Corn Bread

2 lbs black beans
4 medium carrots *(diced)*
2 lg onions *(diced)*
2 each red and green peppers
2 tsp chili powder
2 tsp cumin
1 tsp cajun spice
3 cup tomato paste
7-8 fresh Jalapeno *(sliced)*
Salt & pepper *(to taste)*
sour cream
Monterey cheese *(shredded)*

Soak beans overnight. Drain and cover with fresh water. Bring to boil. Meanwhile, saute onions, carrots, red and green peppers. chili powder, cumin and cajun sauce until tender. Add to beans, cover. Simmer 1 hour, stirring often. Add tomato paste and Jalapenos. Continue to cook at least 90 minutes until beans are *fully, fully* cooked. Best if refrigerated overnight. Serve hot and top with sour cream and shredded Monteray and carrots.

Corn Corn Bread:
1½ cup butter
1½ cup sugar
10 Jalapenos *(diced, seeds removed)*
8 eggs
5 cup flour
4 cups cornmeal
2 tsp baking powder
1 tsp salt
2 cups corn with juice
1½ cup milk

Cream together butter and sugar. Blend in eggs and peppers. Alternate dry ingredients with milk and cron until well mixed. Prepare muffin tins *(grease and flour)* or 9-inch loaf pans. Bake in oven at 350 degrees for 30 minutes. Yields 3 dozen muffins or 4, 9-inch loaves.

Polenta Almond Pound Cake With Fresh Berries

2 cups butter *(softened)*
½ cup almond paste
2½ cup sugar
1 tbls baking powder
1 tsp salt
6 eggs
8 cups flour
2 cups cornmeal
2 cups milk

Blend butter and almond paste. Add eggs and blend until smooth. Alternate milk and dry ingredients until blended. Grease and flour 2, 9 inch loaf pans. Bake each at 350 degrees for 30-40 minutes. Let cool. Remove from pan. Slice and serve topped with fresh berries.

Wine Suggestion

Rye Croft, Chardonnay

2. Zucchini Pie Is Our Fare

On The Menu

Baked Two Cheese Eggplant And Tomato On Herb Pita
Ricotta Zucchini Pie with Garlic Crostini

Crepes with Strawberries AndKiwis with Marscapone Cream

Baked Two Cheese Eggplant And Tomato On Herb Pita

eggplant (¼ inch slices)
egg dip
bread crumbs
olive oil
Mozzarella cheese
Parmesan cheese
oregano
tomatoes
herb pita bread

Slice and soak eggplant for 30 minutes. Drain, pat dry. Place in egg dip, then in bread crumbs. Fry in olive oil until crisp brown. Drain on paper towels. Layer eggplant on parchment-lined sheet pan. Sprinkle with Mozzarella and Parmesan cheeses. Top with tomato and oregano. Repeat once more. Top with Parmesan on final layer. Bake in 375 degree oven for 15-20 minutes. Remove immediately. Slice and place on toasted herb pita triangles. Serve hot.

Ricotta Zucchini Pie with Garlic Crostini

Sauté with garlic, oregano and basil in olive oil:
4 medium zucchinis *(sliced)*
1 onion *(chopped)*
Mix together in bowl:
2 cup Ricotta cheese
1 cup Mozzarella cheese
½ cup Parmesan cheese
2 eggs
1 tsp garlic *(minced)*
Pinch oregano
Pinch basil
Pastry dough:
1½ cup flour
½ cup butter
½ tsp salt
½ tsp sugar
2 tbls water

Pastry dough: Blend butter and dry ingredients. Stir in enough water to make dough meal. Place on large piece of plastic wrap. Fold over ends until they meet. Press down dough. Roll from center until "round." Place in 9 inch pie pan. Layer zucchini mix, then Ricotta. Repeat twice. Top with Mozzarella. Bake at 350 degrees for 60-75 minutes.

Garlic Crostini:
day old Italian bread *(sliced)*
garlic *(minced)*
olive oil

Brush bread with mixture. Broil until lightly browned.

Crepes with Strawberries And Kiwis with Marscapone Cream

Crepes:
1 cup flour
1 tbls sugar
½ tsp cinnamon
2 eggs
½ cup milk
Tossed together:
strawberries *(sliced)*
kiwis *(sliced)*

Blend flour, sugar and cinnamon. Add egg and milk mix. In oiled skillet over medium-high heat, ladle in enough mixture to thinly cover bottom. Turn once. Set aside. Repeat until batter is gone. Fill crepes with strawberries and kiwis. Fold up. Top with mascapone cream. Serve chilled.

Wine Suggestion

Pinot Grigio

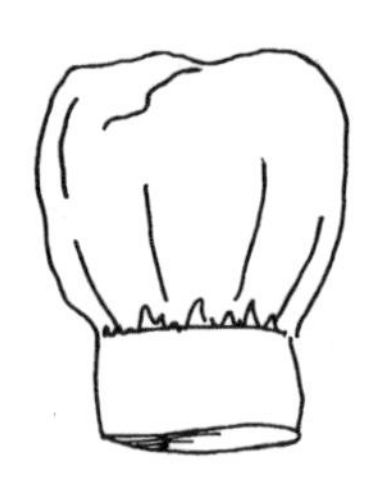

Meet Village Fare Chef Paula Sweeney

Chef Paula Sweeney began working in restaurants while studying at Plymouth State College in New Hampshire. Starting from the ground up, she learned by doing. A gifted and multi-talented Renaissance woman, Paula has also proven herself an accomplished carpenter and roofer. She comes from a family of creative diversity. Her three sisters are also artists, but they agree that Paula is the star of edible art and dough sculpture.

You will find no "chef whites" at the *Village Fare*. No certificates from prestigious culinary institutions. A delightful non-conformist, Paula has the ability to perform 10 tasks well at once. Paula begins her baking at 4 a.m., producing up to 35 different items of breakfast pastries, Danish pies, poured cakes, cookies, brownies, foccacia breads, hard rolls, puff sticks, sticky buns, scones, muffins, to name but a few.

Then it's on to the breakfast menu which includes Eggs Frito Bardito, Granola, Oatmeal and every conceivable omelette on earth. While making breakfast, she is also making three soups and preparing five lunch specials, from smoke salmon and crab cakes to marinated chicken and six or eight salads.

Try the *Village Fare* menus for yourself.

West Mountain Inn

A Country Inn On The Mountainside

On the mountainside in Arlington sits the stately West Mountain Inn. Built as a farmhouse in 1849, the present inn is a result of years of architectural evolution. From 1880 to 1920 it was first a gristmill and later a lumbermill operated alongside the house on the banks of the Battenkill. Ned and Gwendolyn Rochester purchased the 150 acre farm in 1924 and began the renaissance that would transform the farm into an estate suitable for elegant vacationing.

The Rochesters enlarged the house and added the seven gables which remain a prominent feature of the structure today. They dotted the mountainside with barns and small cottages and crisscrossed the hillsides with pastoral stone walls and fences.

A succession of people lived in the estate-like residence following the Rochesters, when in 1978, Wes and Mary Ann Carlson discovered it and knew at once that it could be a haven for them and others as a delightful country inn.

Their skills and philosophy have melded to create an ambience and space that is warm and welcoming. Mary Ann expresses her love of Vermont by serving in the State Senate and has a degree in Holistic Psychology. Wes, known as the resident hug-giver, haunts antique shops and furniture auctions for unique acquisitions.

Guests discover fresh fruit in locally handcrafted pottery bowls as well as Dorothy Canfield Fisher's *Vermont Traditions* awaiting them in their rooms and each guest returns home with an African Violet from the garden, another inn tradition. And, now join Chef Scott Hunt for some culinary delights.

West Mountain Inn, River Road,
Arlington, Vermont 05250 (802) 375-6516

1. Field, Forest And Sea

On The Menu

Pan Seared Scallops With Scallion Cream Sauce
Mesclun Salad With Balsamic Soy Vinaigrette
Sauteéd Tenderloin Of Beef With Chanterelle Mushrooms
With Mushroom Sauce, Scalloped Potatoes, Pan-Glazed Carrots
Cremé Brulee

Pan Seared Scallops With Scallion Cream

20 ea sea scallops *(cleaned of mussels)*
1 oz olive oil
salt, white pepper *(to taste)*

Heat sauté pan. Add olive oil and season scallops with salt and white pepper. Sauté scallops until golden brown.

Scallion Cream Sauce:
1 cup white wine
2 scallions *(rough chopped)*
1½ oz shallots *(rough chopped)*
1½ oz garlic *(rough chopped)*
1 ea thyme *(whole sprigs)*
1 pint heavy cream
2 oz butter *(cubed)*
salt, white pepper *(to taste)*
1 oz olive oil

In saucepan, sweat (slightly sauté) shallots, garlic, thyme. Add scallions and sweat until limp. Add white wine until al sec *(almost dry)*. Add pepper. Purée, adding small amounts of butter until finished. Strain.

Mesclun Salad With Balsamic Soy Vinaigrette

1 cup olive oil
2/3 cup balsamic vinegar
1/3 cup soy sauce
1 oz garlic *(minced)*
1 oz shallots *(minced)*
2 sprigs thyme *(chopped)*
2 sprigs parsley *(chopped)*
salt, white pepper *(to taste)*
1 lb mesclun salad
8 slices European cucumber *(sliced thin)*
8 cherry tomatoes *(sliced in middle, not separated)*
6-8 radishes *(shaved)* 1-2 carrots *(shaved)*
salt and white pepper *(to taste)*

Let garlic, shallots, thyme, parsley steep in the balsamic soy for 2 hours. Slowly whip the olive oil into the vinegar mix. Season with salt and pepper. Garnish salad with cherry tomatoes, sliced European cukes, shaved carrots and shaved radishes.

Sautéed Tenderloin Of Beef With Chanterelle Mushrooms And Scalloped Potatoes

8, 4 oz tenderloins *(cleaned)*
salt and pepper
1 oz olive oil

Season tenderloin of beef. Sauté until desired degree of doneness. Set aside.

Chanterelle Sauce:
1 oz olive oil
1 oz shallots *(diced)*
1 sprig thyme *(chopped)*
2-3 sprigs parsely *(chopped)*
10-12 oz demi-glaze
salt and white pepper
1 oz butter *(cubed)*
2-3 oz hydrated chanterelle mushrooms
4-5 oz merlot wine

In saucepan, sweat garlic, shallots, thyme, parsley. Add merlot wine until al sec. Add demi-glaze and reduce until desired thickness of sauce. Strain sauce through chinoix *(strainer)*. Whip butter into sauce. Add chanterelle mushrooms. Season with salt and white pepper.

Scalloped Potatoes:
18-20 red bliss potatoes *(washed, par boiled, sliced ½ inch thick)*
1 pint heavy cream
3-4 oz Parmesan cheese *(grated)*
3 sprigs thyme *(chopped)*
1 ea Vedalia onions *(french cut)*
2 ea scallions *(cut on bias, small)*
salt, white pepper *(to taste)*

Layer potatoes in 2 inch high square pan. Sprinkle Parmesan cheese, onions, scallions, thyme, parsley on top. Mix all together. Season with salt, white pepper and bake in 350 degree oven for 35-40 minutes. Take out of oven and reserve for plating presentation.

Pan Glazed Carrots:
1 lb carrots (cleaned and sliced in rings)
½ cup Vermont maple syrup

2 tbls brown sugar
pinch of ginger

Boil carrots until barely tender *(about 5 minutes)*. Drain dry. Combine all ingredients in frying pan and sauté 5 minutes. Put frying pan in oven at 350 degrees for 10 minutes. Serve immediately.

Cremé Brulee

½ pint heavy cream
2 egg yolks
1½ oz sugar
½ vanilla bean

Heat cream, add sugar with vanilla bean, temper yolks, mix. Pour through chinoix. Remove foam with ladle. Bake in ramiken in pan of water in oven at 250 degrees until golden brown and texture is firm. Remove from oven. Chill and serve with Creme Anglaise.

Creme Anglaise:
8 egg yolks
2 eggs *(whole)*
½ pint milk; ½ pint heavy cream *(or quart of half and half)*
2/3 lb granulated sugar
½ vanilla bean *(split down seam)*

Put cream and milk in a pan on the fire. Get eggs ready. Put ½ sugar into milk and cream mixture. Mix sugar and eggs well. Add vanilla bean to milk, cream mixture. When milk gets hot, temper the eggs. Bring milk to boil and add eggs. Strain into bowl in ice bath. Stir constantly, keeping chilled.

Wine Suggestion

Merlot, Clos du Bois

2. Berries And Mountain Maple On The Menu

Curried Chicken Phyllo Puffs
Spinach Salad With West Mountain Inn Maple Dill Dressing
Aunt Min's Rye Bread
Pan Seared Pork Tenderloin With Wild Berry Sauce,
Pomme Gratin Dauphinoise, Braised Red Cabbage and Green Beans
Creme de Chocolat Pie

Curried Chicken Phyllo Puffs

8 oz chicken *(cut into small pieces)*
½ onion *(diced small)*
2 tbls garlic *(freshly minced)*
2 tbls madras curry

1/8 cup slivered almonds
4 oz softened cream cheese
1/8 cup raisins
clarified butter
soy sauce *(to taste)*

Sauté until onions are translucent. Add soy sauce to taste. Sauté or poach 8 oz chicken. Add slivered almonds and raisins. Blend into cream cheese.

Place one sheet of phyllo dough on wax paper. Brush lightly with clarified butter. Repeat for four layers. Cut dough into 2 inch strips with sharp knife. Place 1-2 tbls chicken mixture in one corner and fold like a flag *(3 times over)* to create a triangle. Repeat steps until desired quantity is achieved. Bake at 450 degrees for about 12-15 minutes or until brown.

Spinach Salad With West Mountain Inn Maple Dill Dressing

Dressing:
¼ cup maple syrup
¼ cup balsamic vinegar
3 tsp dill
1 tsp parsley *(minced...optional)*
Dash salt and pepper
2 egg yolks
2 cups oil
8 cherry tomatoes
8 cucumbers

Combine all ingredients except oil in blender and mix on low speed. Gradually add oil, pouring in very slowly to avoid separation. Makes approximately 2½ cups dressing. Serve over fresh spinach with cucumbers, cherry tomatoes, radishes and shaved carrots.

Aunt Min's Rye Bread

1 cup warm water
2 tbls yeast
½ cup melted butter
2 eggs
¼ cup brown sugar
pinch salt
¼ cup fennel seeds
¼ cup molasses
1 cup rye flour
3-4 cups white flour

Combine warm water and yeast and let stand 5 minutes. Add melted butter and eggs *(room temperature)*. Add remaining ingredients to this mixture. Add rye flour and use white flour to achieve the consistency of bread dough.

Proof dough until doubled in size. Form into 3, 1 lb loaves and place in greased loaf pans. Proof again and double in size. Bake in 350 degree oven approximately 20-30 minutes until done.

Pan Seared Pork Tenderloin
With Wild Berry Sauce,
Pomme Gratin Dauphinoise, Braised Red Cabbage and Green Beans

8, 8 oz. pork tenderloin
1 oz olive oil
salt, white pepper *(to taste)*

In a sauté pan with oil, sear pork tenderloin. Put in pre-heated oven at 375 degrees to desired doneness.

Wild Berry Sauce:

1 oz olive oil
1 oz shallots *(rough chop)*
1 oz garlic *(rough chop)*
1 sprig thyme *(rough chop)*
4-5 oz cabernet sauvignon
10-12 oz demi-glaze
1 oz butter *(cubed)*
2 oz lingonberries
1 oz cranberries
1 oz blueberries

In saucepan, sweat shallots, garlic, thyme, parsley with olive oil. Add cabernet sauvignon and reduce al sec. Add demi-glaze and reduce by half. Strain through chinoix, add berries and drain. Monte au buerre. Season with salt, pepper.

Pomme Gratin Dauphinoise:
15-20 Idaho potatoes *(peeled, sliced, but not ruined)*
1 pint heavy cream
4 eggs
2 ea garlic *(chopped)*
salt and white pepper *(to taste)*
nutmeg *(to taste)*

In square pan, layer potatoes tightly together. Mix all ingredients together and pour over potatoes. Bake in 350 degree oven until potatoes are cooked to satisfaction. Cool, then cut to desired shape.

Green Beans:
julienne red peppers
mushrooms *(sliced)*
almonds *(toasted)*
oil

Blanch green beans 6-8 minutes in boiling salt water. Drain and set aside. Combine peppers, mushrooms and almonds and sauté in oil. Add mixture to beans, season with salt and pepper and serve.

Sautéed Red Cabbage:
1 head red cabbage
1 cup red wine
½ cup brown sugar
salt, white pepper *(to taste)*
thyme
sesame seeds
olive oil

In large sauté pan, add olive oil, red cabbage. Cook for 20 minutes. Add red wine. Let reduce to al sec *(almost dry)*. Add brown sugar, thyme, sesame seeds. Cook for 3 minutes. Adjust seasoning and steam out excess liquid.

Creme de Chocolat Pie

3 cups whole milk
3 oz chocolate *(unsweetened)*
1 cup sugar
3 egg yolks
¼ cup cornstarch
1 tsp vanilla
1 tsp butter
4, 8-inch pastry or graham cracker pie shells

Blend milk, chocolate, sugar, egg yolks, cornstarch. Stir with whisk constantly over medium heat until mixture thickens. Add vanilla and butter. Pour into 8 inch pastry or graham cracker pie shell. Serve with dollop of fresh, whipped cream.

Wine Suggestion

Cabernet Sauvignon, Hirsch Estate

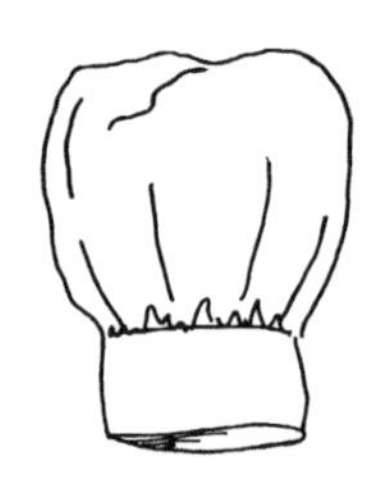

Meet Inn At West Mountain Chef Scott Hunt

Chef Scott Hunt is a graduate of the New England Culinary Institute in Montpelier, Vermont and has been involved in a variety of kitchen assignments with restaurants throughout New England. He comes to the Inn At West Mountain from the Monks Inn Restaurant in Bethel, Maine, where he served as head chef. Prior to that, Chef Hunt worked with the Ritz Carlton hotels in their Palm Beach, Florida and Boston, Massachusetts properties.

His other Massachusetts experiences include the Boston Harbor Hotel, Daniel Fuller House in Middleton, Cherrystones in Danvers, Ron BurtonTraining Village in Hubbardston, Jesters Court Cafe at the Sheraton Tara Hotel in Danvers and Crosby's Marketplace in Salem to develop his fine produce knowledge.

Chef Hunt took second place honors in Culinary Arts School Competition in 1987 and 1988 and won two achievement awards. He received the Ron Burton Award for Outstanding Culinary Preparation in 1987.

Wilburton Inn

A Truly Romantic Setting

Like all truly romantic settings, the history of the Wilburton Inn is a combination of fact and fantasy. It begins with a Vermont farmer who won a parcel of land in a poker game and continues in Chicago, where Albert Gilbert and Robert Todd Lincoln, the President's son, decided to create two neighboring Vermont estates.

Gilbert's architect blended a European Tudor style with the new modernism promoted by Frank Lloyd Wright. The mansion sits on a hill overlooking the Battenkill River. When Gilbert died in 1906, his banker, James Wilbur, purchased the estate and renamed it Wilburton Hall.

Wilbur was a self-made millionaire from Cleveland who had been Cashier of the New Haven Railroad and then President of a powerful Chicago bank. Yet, he had a profound love of Vermont. His generous donations to the University of Vermont included the elegant Ira Allen Chapel and a scholarship worth more than $6 million. He came to Vermont each summer and motored around Europe in the fall. He died in 1928, and when the family fortune declined, he explained it to his son this way: "There is Money and there is money."

The estate was leased to a private school during World War II, where many of the students were children of European diplomats and creative artists who had fled from the Nazis. Wilburton Hall became Wilburton Inn in 1945 and the tony clientele of sporting gentlemen skied, golfed and wagered. During the 1970s the hotel was purchased by General Tire/R.K.O. and the Inn was primarily used for corporate entertaining and as a summer and fall resort.

Dr. Albert Levis and his family came to the inn for his birthday in 1987 and three months later they purchased it. A Greek born psychiatrist, his collection of art and scupture is displayed throughout the inn. Innkeeper Georgette Levis is the sister of financier Bruce Wasserstein, executive Sandra Meyer and acclaimed playwright Wendy Wasserstein. The Levis family includes four children. Vermonter Stan Holton is general manager, while his wife Lucille is head housekeeper. She once modeled for Norman Rockwell when he worked and lived in nearby Arlington.

Chef David Stoel, whose dinner recipes follow, creates the wonderful meals enjoyed at the Inn. A specialty is country weddings, corporate retreats and happy events.

Wilburton Inn, River Road, Manchester Village, Vermont 05254
(802) 362-2500; (800) 648-4944

1. Dog Days Of August Barbecue For Six

On The Menu

Chevre And Chive Rolls
Chilled Cucumber Dill Soup
Nappa Salad With Raspberry Dressing, Red Bell Pepper And Toasted Cashews
Charbroiled Marinated Butterflied Leg Of Lamb With Grilled Marinated Vegetables And Garlic Roasted Red Bliss Potatoes
Peachtrree White Peach Sorbet

Chevre And Chive Rolls

2 tsp (½ oz) yeast *(dry)*
1½ cup water *(warm)*
1 tbls King Arthur all-purpose flour
¼ cup (2 oz) brown sugar *(packed)*
1 egg
1½ tsp (½ oz) salt
½ cup corn oil
2 tsp chives *(chopped)*
½ cup (4 oz) chevre *(packed)*
½ (2½ oz) corn meal
6 cups (1 lb, 13 oz) King Arthur A.P. flour
Egg Wash:
1 egg
1 tbls water

In a mixing bowl, proof yeast in water with brown sugar and flour. Add egg, salt, oil, chives, chevre and whisk. Using break hook, mix dough about 10 minutes until smooth and elastic. Add more flour sparingly if sticky.

Cover bowl with damp cloth and plastic wrap and let rise until double in volume. Punch dough down and turn from bowl onto floured surface. Scale dough into two ounce units.Round each unit. Place rolls two inches apart on lightly greased sheet pan. Brush with egg wash. Let rise till almost double in volume. Bake in preheated 375-degree oven until golden brown. Yields 25 rolls.

Chilled Cucumber Dill Soup

3 cups buttermilk
½ cups sour cream
2 cups cucumber *(skinned, seeded, chopped)*
¼ cup dill *(fresh, chopped)*
¼ cup rice wine vinegar
½ tsp garlic *(fresh, chopped)*
1 tsp Durkee hot sauce
salt *(to taste)*
In a bowl, combine ingredients together and chill.

Nappa Cabbage With Raspberry Dressing And Red Bell Pepper

Salad:
2 heads nappa cabbage *(shredded)*
1 red bell pepper *(julienne)*
1 cup toasted cashew
Dressing:
1 egg
½ cup raspberry vinegar
½ cup raspberry pureee
1 tsp salt
½ tsp white pepper
2 cups corn oil

Salad: Combine cabbage, red pepper and cashews in a bowl.

Dressing: In a bowl, combine first five ingredients. Slowly whisk in oil.

Char-broiled Marinated Butterflied Leg Of Lamb

1 butterflied leg of lamb
8 oz bottle of poupon mustard
6 oz red wine vinegar
16 oz olive oil
1 tsp fresh rosemary *(finely chopped)*
1 tsp sage *(rubbed)*
6-8 garlic cloves *(chopped)*
salt and pepper *(to taste)*

Cut lamb into manageable pieces along seam lines. Combine all ingredients except lamb into a bowl and stir until well blended. Add lamb to marinate. Cover and refrigerate for two hours. Remove from marinade and grill or barbecue to your desired temperature.

Grilled Marinated Vegetables:
3 medium zucchini
3 summer squash
3 red bell peppers
Marinate:
¼ cup lemon juice
1 cup extra virgin olive oil
1 tbls fresh oregano
1 tbls fresh basil
salt and pepper to taste

Cut vegetables about 3/8 of an inch thick on a bias. Cut red peppers in half and remove seeds. Continue cutting in pieces large enough not to fall through grill. Toss vegetables in marinate for 10 minutes. Grill about 2 minutes on each side.

Garlic Roasted New Potatoes:
2 lbs red bliss potatoes *(grade b)*

¼ cup fresh garlic (chopped)
¼ cup fresh rosemary (chopped)
salt and pepper to taste
½ cup extra virgin olive oil

Parboil potatoes in enough water to completely cover them. Add water if necessary during cooking process. Drain water from potatoes when done. Let cool. Combine garlic, rosemary, salt, pepper, and olive oil. Gently toss the potatoes in the mixture and finish cooking potatoes in a roasting pan in the oven.

Peachtree White Peach Sorbet

1 quart white peach pulp
1 lb super fine sugar
1 quart water
¼ cup Peachtree

Mix together the four ingredients. Place in ice cream machine to process following manufacturer's instructions. Remove from machine when firm. Place in freezer for at least four hours before using.

Wine Suggestion

Pinot Noir, Acacia Carneros

2. Cool Autumn Evening

Dinner For Six

On The Menu

Wilburton Focaccia
Savory Portabella Tart
Boston Bib Lettuce With Maple Mustard Dressing
Oven Roasted Duckling With Cointreau Orange Sauce
Wild Rice
Broccoli With Hazelnut Brown Butter
Caramel Custard

Wilburton Focaccia

2 tsp dry yeast
1 cup warm water
1 tbls King Arthur all-purpose flour
1 tsp brown sugar
1¼ cups warm water
¼ cup virgin olive oil
2 tsp fresh rosemary (chopped)
1 tbls scallions (chopped)
1 tbls koshered salt

pinch of ground black pepper
8 cups King Arthur all-purpose flour
extra virgin olive oil *(for brushing and kosher salt for sprinkling on loaves)*

Proof yeast using ¼ cup water, sugar and tablespoon flour in a mixing bowl. Add remaining water, oil, rosemary, scallions, salt, pepper and whisk. Using bread hook, mix dough about 10 minutes.

Cover bowl with a damp cloth and plastic wrap and place in a warm area to rise. When the dough has doubled in volume, punch down and turn from bowl onto a lightly floured surface.

Divide dough into four units. Round each unit and place on lightly oiled sheet pan. Using finger tips, press dough down to about ½ inch thick. Brush with olive oil and sprinkle surface with a tsp of koshered salt. *Do not let rise.* Bake immediately in a pre-heated 375 degree oven for 20 minutes or until loaves have a hollow sound when tapped.

Savory Portabello Tart

Crust:
1½ cup all-purpose flour
½ tsp salt
½ cup chilled butter *(cut into pieces)*
2 tbls ice water

In a food processor, mix salt and flour. Add butter, pulse processor until mixture looks like coarse meal. Add just enough water to form dough. Remove from machine and refrigerate for at least 30 minutes.

Roll dough out to fit a 10-inch tart pan. Chill for thirty minutes. Cover crust with parchment paper and fill with dry beans. Bake in oven at 350 degrees for 10 minutes. Remove foil and beans. Brush with egg whites and return to oven. Bake until golden.

Filling:
1 lb Portabello mushrooms *(trimmed and sliced)*
1/3 cup shallots *(chopped)*
½ cup extra virgin olive oil
¼ cup Grand Armagnac
1 tbls Provence dry herbs with fennel
8 oz Dill Havarti *(grated)*
8 oz Vermont chevre
1 cup cream
3 egg yolks
1 egg

Heat a sauté pan and add olive oil. When the oil is hot, add mushrooms and shallots; cook until the mushrooms have lost most of their moisture. Add herbs and salt, then the Armagnac.

In a bowl, mix the cream, egg yolks, egg, and chevre. Combine this with the cooked mushrooms. Spread the grated dill Havrati on the finished crust. Add the cheese and mushroom filling. Bake in 350 degree oven for 20 to 30 minutes or until filling is firm to touch and top is golden brown.

Oven Roasted Duckling With Cointreau Orange Sauce

3, 6 lb fresh Long Island ducklings
3 oranges *(cut in half)*
3 tsp salt
3 tbls fresh rosemary *(chopped)*
1 lb carrots *(sliced in half, lengthwise)*
6 stalks celery

Duck stock:
bones from cooked ducklings
carrots and celery used in roasting
2 quarts cold water

Simmer stock slowly until liquid is reduced by half. Strain, cool, skim fat.

Preparation of duckling: Preheat oven to 350 degrees. Remove neck and organ packet from duck cavity. Rinse with cold water. Remove outer two wing sections and cut excess fat from neck and tail. Salt cavity and place rosemary and orange halves inside. Arrange carrots, celery, neck and wing joints in a high-sided roasting pan so the neck will rest above the rendered fat. Pour about ¼ inch of water into bottom of pan to keep from burning. Add more water carefully during cooking process if needed.

Place duck in pre-heated oven for about 3 hours. Remove and let cool. Split in half and remove all bones except the remaining wing joint and drum stick. *(These bones and the roasted carrots and celery are used for the duck stock.)* Just before serving, duck halves are placed skin side up in a pan with a small amount of water into a 450 degree oven for about 8 minutes to crisp skin.

Cointreau Orange Sauce:
¼ cup cider vinegar
¼ cup granulated sugar
1½ cups orange juice
1½ cups duck stock
½ cup orange marmalade
2 tbls Cointreau
6 tsp Wondra Flour

In a sauce pan, place the sugar and vinegar and carmelize with moderate heat. When medium brown color is obtained, carefully and immediately pour orange juice and duck stock into the pan. Add the marmalade and Cointreau. Simmer for five minutes and thicken with Wondra.

Boston Bibb Lettuce With Maple Mustard Dressing

3 heads Boston Bibb lettuce
1 egg
2 tbls dijon mustard
1 tsp salt
½ tsp ground black pepper
1 cup corn oil

¼ cup cider vinegar
1/3 cup maple syrup

Clean lettuce heads in cold water and discard unsatisfactory leaves. Arrange on chilled plates. Combine egg and mustard in bowl with a whip. Add slowly to this oil to make an emulsion. Whip in remaining ingredients. Ladle on lettuce.

Wild Rice

1½ cups wild rice
6 cups boiling water
1 tsp salt
4 strips cob smoked bacon *(julienne)*
½ cup celery *(chopped)*
½ cup onion *(chopped)*
1 tsp thyme
salt and pepper to taste

Wash rice in cold water and drain. Stir rice slowly into boiling water. Cook 30-40 minutes without stirring until rice puffs. Drain. Sauté bacon until crisp, then remove from pan. Using the rendered bacon fat, cook the celery and onions until tender. Add thyme, salt and pepper. Cook a few minutes longer, then add the drained rice.

Broccoli With Hazlenut Brown Butter

3 heads broccoli
1 tsp salt
boiling water *(sufficient to cover broccoli)*
ice water
½ cup hazelnuts *(chopped)*
½ cup butter
¼ cup water

Trim broccoli and cook in salted water until tender. Drain, then shock broccoli in an ice bath to retain a bright green color. Place butter and hazlenuts in a skillet, cook over high heat until butter starts to brown. Immediately add the cooked broccoli to pan and the water. Warm and coat broccoli in pan with the butter and nut sauce.

Caramel Custard

Custard:
7 eggs
3 cups milk
6 oz sugar
1½ tsp vanilla extract
Caramel:
1 cup water
1 cup sugar

Caramel: Combine ½ cup water with all the sugar in a sauce pan. Have reserved water within immediate reach. Cook sugar water until medium amber in color. Carefully add reserved water. Heat about 5 minutes longer until the added water has combined with the syrup and has thickened. Pour syrup into soup cups and cool.

Custard: Scald the milk in a sauce pan. Combine the eggs, sugar, and vanilla in a bowl and whisk together. Slowly add the scalded milk to the egg mixture, stirring constantly. Remove froth. Ladle custard into soup cups. Place soup cups in a pan suitable for a water bath that will enable you to fill the pan with hot water to within ¼ inch of the top of the cups. Bake the custard in a pre-heated 350 degree oven for about 45 minutes or until custard is firm to touch. Cool. Loosen custard from sides of the cup with a knife. Invert on individual plates. Garnish with berries.

Wine Suggestion

Rosemont Estate Chardonnay

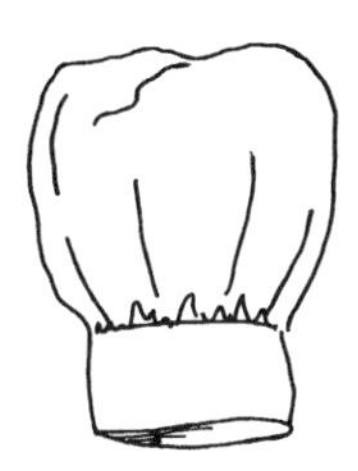

Meet Wilburton Inn Chef David A. Stoel

Chef David Stoel first began working in restaurants while attending college and discovering that the cafeteria food was terrible. He was studying Marine Science at the time at Southampton College. He came to Vermont to work under Master Chef Anton Flay at The Topnotch At Stowe.

His New York cooking career includes Dillons in Southampton, Westhampton Country Club in Westhampton and LeRound Beach Club in Westhampton Beach.

Here in Vermont, Chef Stoel was a line cook at Villa Targara in Waterbury Center, Swing Chef at Top Notch and Swing Chef at Mount Mansfield Resort at Stowe before arriving at the *Wilburton Inn* in 1990.

An outdoor sportsman, he participates in alpine and cross country skiing, snowshoeing, hunting, kyaking, canoeing, scuba diving, biking, travel and hiking.

Chef Stoel enjoys eating as much as cooking and takes great pleasure in sitting down and eating a home-cooked meal prepared by someone else.

Professional wisdom, Chef Stoel style, is "you are only as good as your staff," so he invites all to revisit the *Wilburton Inn* and enjoy dinner and the fine staff who prepate and serve it.

Mountain Stirrings Makes A Wonderful Gift For Any Occasion!

To order additional copies, send $14.95 per book plus $4 for priority shipping up to 3 books *(add 50 cents per additional book),* to:

Marshall Jones Co.
P.O. Box 2327
Manchester Center, VT 05255

Or Call:
(800) 258-1505
(802) 362-5066